Many blessings in return,

xoxo

Yassin Hall

Beyond the Love Curse

Own Your Power

As told to

Co-author Brenda Green

FIRST EDITION

PREFACE

In this introspective, riveting, insightful autobiographical memoir, Yassin credits her beloved 93-year-old Granny (Mama's) unconditional love and wisdom for giving her the endurance and strength to overcome all that life has dealt her.

Hall is authentic, transparent and raw as she shares the many facets of her dynamic life and colorful personality. The chapters are like peeling an onion as Hall deftly delivers the most dismal times of her life.

Readers will experience so many emotions, but in the end will be cheering for Hall's escape, redemption, and power to rebuild a successful life.

She unapologetically takes the reader on her journey to find peace, joy and wholeness. Hall, an advocate and champion of mental wellness finally realizes that hurt and broken people hurt and break others.

Hall reveals, "I sought answers from others about my own value. I did not see nor know that I was born valuable," but continuous talk therapy has helped her to let go of shame, anxiety and self-hate and walk proudly in her truth. She challenges readers to own their power and to unabashedly live their reality with no regrets.

Today, she is vulnerable enough and ready to expend the energy to try emotional intimacy to break the love curse because she knows that if Love fails her again and again, she is built and equipped to survive.

Praise for Yassin Hall's Beyond the Love Curse

Yassin Hall's "Beyond the Love Curse" the much-anticipated sequel to her first novel "Journey Untold - My Mother's Struggle with Mental Illness", did not disappoint! Ms. Hall goes deep and bares her soul about a life that has experienced more tragedy than any one person should. Her introspection of her life's events speaks to the soul and serves as an inspiration to others that may be living through similar circumstances. The novel's open, candid and therapeutic nature will make it a prize winner for sure.

~ Emani Emanuel

The author opens up and shows the reader her vulnerability and weaknesses and how she overcame them. The author gives the reader enough information for them to draw their own conclusions and take from the book what they need. The main idea is supported by viewpoints and many readers will find they can relate.

Yassin lets the readers see her from the inside out, this story not just about her. Hall gives the readers helpful advice as to how to climb out of the trenches when it feels as if you are falling into the abyss. Her message is clear: Sometimes the roller coaster ride is best viewed from the ground. Like a car too tattered to withstand another wreck, Hall moved out of the hammer lane and into the slow lane where she could take control once again. The readers will see this and appreciate that they, too, can do it.

~ Carol Thompson – Readers Favorites

Yassin gives us a graphic look at her life, overcoming obstacles, family difficulties, disappointments and pleasure.

She shows us her vulnerabilities throughout her emotional journey to being content. Her strength and determination will help encourage others to tell their truth and owning their own peace.

~ Ivy Ferris

This book is a must read. From the moment I began reading, I was hooked the introduction as it brought tears in my eyes. I knew at that point; it was going to be amazing. This book was very uplifting, empowering, and motivational. I felt like it was written just for me, I related to every part. There were several things I took notes of so I can remember it in the future, the five questions that a person should ask their self before reacting. The affirmations Yassin listed to tell yourself when your power is disturbed are two of the things I am starting to practice in my life. This book helped me heal and grow. It will do the same for so many people who are hurting.

~ Jejetta Lee

This book was truly an O.M.G. book that I could not put down. (I didn't want to!) I don't think I have ever read a book in 3 hours. It had me experiencing all the different emotions and touched me beyond words. I was laughing, crying, experiencing anger, and just mesmerized by the words in this book. It is a Journey of love, complications, truth and reality. This book is a testimony to all women who have experienced these events in their lives. Thank YOU Yassin, for allowing me to enter YOUR world and getting to know you inside and out through Beyond The Love Curse. ~ Nicole Lowe

Married life was a blessing and very tough at the same time. Hey, it didn't kill us, and we are stronger now.

~ Mark Young

Connect with me

www.YassinHall.com

www.BOSSAmazonClass.com

m.me/YassinHall (Messenger)

https://www.linkedin.com/in/yassinhall/

https://www.facebook.com/yassinshall

https://www.instagram.com/yassinhall/

https://www.instagram.com/journeyuntold/

https://twitter.com/journeyuntold

bookyassinhall@gmail.com

678-870-4099

I would love to hear from my readers please feel free to leave a review on my Amazon Author Page:

https://www.amazon.com/Yassin-Hall/e/B00TT5F0A2

This book is dedicated to:

My God-Loving ninety-three-year-old Granny Delia Simmonds. In my eyes, you are the epitome of the strength of a million women. Although I am still growing every day, the things in life I have watched you endure have made me the woman, with only half of your strength, that I am today. You turned my words of "I can't get through this" into "With God's mighty strength I shall," and I have. You have been there for every fall and every great moment in my life. You have shown me unwavering and unconditional love. I love you to infinity times infinity, and I am ever so thankful to God for choosing you to be the woman who nurtured me. Thank you for never allowing me to give up. With every prayer you've delivered to God on my behalf, I now realize how truly powerful of a woman I am. I love you.

Your loving granddaughter,

Yassin S. Hall

Table of Contents

Prelude

The best LOVE is the kind that awakens the soul; that makes us reach for more, that plants a fire in our hearts and brings peace to our minds. That's what I hope to bring you forever. - The Notebook

This is my all-time favorite quote. This is my vision of what love looks like in this present time.

The love I'm referring to is not receptive love from someone; I'm talking about self-love.

In my opinion, self-love is defined by understanding, knowing, and truly believing you are worthy of the energy, time and positive aspects in your life that bring you internal joy. A joy that can be seen in your eyes and the lovely glow on your skin that illuminates pure radiance and makes others around you want to be in your presence because they, too, want to feel such joy.

Self-love involves deep healing, fulfilling your emotions and realigning your mental state of mind.

To begin to love yourself, you must know that you are created from love and own that love from the higher power in the universe.

Self-love isn't selfish; it's necessary. It's healthy to love yourself. Loving yourself has everything to do with self-respect, self-actualization, and choosing joy for yourself and your life. Self-love is the greatest form of compassion because it opens your heart to know you're perfect in God's eyes just the way you are.

Self-love has no conditions. Many times, we put conditions on the love we give and receive. We say things like, "When I get a good man, I'll be happy" ..."When I hit my goal weight, I'll feel satisfied" ...."When I build my bank account and buy all the things I want, I'll be content." Being stuck in the "when" moments prevent you from feeling joy...When that moment passes, you are right back into setting more conditions.

Self-love is unconditional, and it's being comfortable loving your skin. A person who has true self-love works at finding balance and joy. The key ingredient to knowing you have self-love is feeling joy. Joy is the ultimate version of infinite happiness. When you are in a joyful place in your life, you "own your power!" A woman who has self-love is the most powerful element of existence. She is unstoppable.

I didn't always think of love this way. For the majority of my life, I felt unlovable. No, scratch that. I knew that I was unlovable and kept asking myself why do I hurt so deeply from love? I sought answers from others about my own value. I did not see nor know that I was born valuable.

How could I not think that? My mother never told me she loved me. In *Journey Untold,* you read about the dreadful day: the day she wanted to end my young life. Come on, let's face it. Even my own father didn't love me nor want me. When the man who should be your first love doesn't love you, then who will? These thoughts stayed and resonated with me for over forty-plus years.

Sadly, millions of fatherless girls must have had this thought at least once in their lives, although they may not express it out loud. I know I would never have.

Here I am, once again opening more chapters of my life, my hopes, and goals to inspire women around the world to find joy within themselves. Come take a journey with me. I had to discover myself or continue to depend on other people's opinions of who I was. It's funny, but those same people don't even know themselves.

On this journey, I will guide you deeper into the relationships I've been in and share the lessons I've learned that taught me how to stop behaviors that I couldn't see in myself. I knew I needed help to avoid any further mental harm. I'll also share coping methods that I use as I continue to heal through my mental wellness journey.

I'm owning my power by writing my truth; I'm free.

Introduction

I entered the world as a female. Like most women, we want that baby girl–our legacy child. For mothers, it's a pure moment of joy in hearing the words, "It's a girl." It makes us forget that we are born into an unjust world, labeled, and objectified because we are women. It's as if it's written on our foreheads in invisible ink. It doesn't make it wrong or right; it's a fact.

Alicia Stout, one of my Facebook Friends, said, "Yassin, a woman's feminine parts should be named "Divine Feminine." That is exactly what it is. Girl, listen...

We are alchemists.

We move souls from heaven to earth, changing essence/spirit into what is tangible/corporeal.

We change tears into smiles, fears into fight, and ignorance into knowledge.

We provide comfort, coverage, and a safe haven.

We can create and/or destroy with our words, thoughts, and touch.

When you consider the inherent beauty, strength, resilience, and fortitude of our feminine selves, how could it not be divine?"

Reading this made me pause, exhale, and embrace the *woman* within. Did you not feel the same way?

Many times in life, people will question our sanity and degrade our vagina. When this happens, it simply means, from my experience, I'm gaining too much power and that's their way of attempting to lower my self-love. I've never let them take my power.

In today's world, no matter if you do a million things right, humans will sit and wait until you do something wrong or they will listen to something said negatively about you. This isn't for or about you; don't take it personally. It's so they can feel better about their pathetic lives, so just keep living your life.

Society wants us all to believe that being mentally unstable, or even a whore, is *ultimately* the worst thing a woman can be. And without looking into their browned-grass backyards, they believe that the pleasure of experiencing multiple relationships along your life's journey is unethical.

Says who?

Internal Self Thoughts: *I don't think a woman's actions who stands up for herself because she knows her worth should be viewed as worse than that of a mass murderer, rapist or priest molesting or having sex with boys. Mass murderers—Are they usually men or women? Hmmm. . . Mass murderers are categorized as having a "mental illness." Yet, women are the "crazy" ones...?*

The truth is that when another person attacks your mental state and/or sexuality, then they have unknowingly relinquished their power to you. What you do with that power is a reflection of who you are as a woman.

I want others to learn from me how to handle their reactions to these situations.

It's not what was said or done to you that truly counts. It's how you react in these situations that will resonate in people's minds and show how it feels to "own your power." That's why it's so important not to let your emotions lead your actions. I know in most situations it's hard to not get emotional. Lies are told. Stories are twisted. It's your truth versus someone else's. It's your word against another's. I get it.

Many times, as women we respond, and the situation becomes worse. The end result is regret and self-hatred compounded with self-doubt. I know because I'm guilty. This is a vicious cycle, but no one has really taught us differently, or so we think. We were told by our grandparents, parents, aunts, cousins, etc. We just weren't listening.

Let me give you an example from my experience. My first-born was shot five times in the back by a young man who hung out just two doors down from my maternal grandmother's house. This young man left my son to die, lying in his blood. Fortunately, my son survived with no physical deformities.

During a visit to my hometown, St. Thomas, United States Virgin Islands, while visiting my grandmother, she was baking a cake for the young man who shot my son.

I walked outside behind her as she told me, "Come, let's go."

She stopped and stood in front of him, prayed for him, and told him to repent to God for his sins. She did this with no fear.

My grandmother told him to go back to school, learn a trade, and stay off the streets.

I was standing behind her as the mother of the child this young man tried to kill. In fury, thinking, "Let me have him for an hour in a closed room, please and thank you." I was also thinking that it was some serious God's love that I didn't have at all. I was hurt, and hurt people tend to want to hurt others for that moment of justice. That's what the mother in me wanted to feel in that moment. Yet, I did nothing. I gazed at her, thinking *this woman is nuts*! I was scratching my head thinking, "Who does this?" I didn't realize that at that moment that my grandmother had shown me what owning your own power looks like. She never said, "Yassin, this is what power looks like." She just turned away, walked back to her house, up the stairs, and turned on the radio like it was nothing.

I was walking behind her thinking, "Okay then, this is different." I also thought I was going to have to lock my granny in a crazy-ward one day! You see, her reaction was of God's doing, and I didn't understand or comprehend the lesson.

Months later, I called my grandmother and asked her a ton of questions. My mind was ever so curious, or maybe subconsciously I wanted to learn such restraint from her.

I asked, "Ma, this young man shot your great-grandson and left him to die. Yet, you baked him a cake?"

She responded, "I've always baked him a cake every year; he loved my sweetbread." I taught that young man in first grade. Yes, what he did was wrong, but who am I to judge? That's for God to do. My job is to forgive and pray for his soul here on earth.

Her answer resonated with me from that day onward.

Less than a week later, this young man was shot multiple times in the back and slowly bled to death, lying in his blood.

When I spoke to my grandmother, I could hear the hurt she had for him. She paused, and said, "God knew best. I hope he repented while he suffered." She then prayed for his family.

I'm not perfect, and I'm learning through therapy how to hold onto my power in every life situation. For me to be eternally happy with the woman I choose to become, I choose to no longer be guilty of giving another person that much power over my emotions. Learn the 5X5 Rule. If it's not going to affect your future in the next five years, don't spend more than five minutes of your emotions on it.

Take a moment before you react. You hold the power of your outcome. Ask yourself these five questions:

1. Is your reaction worth your energy and time? Do you not have anything more important to do?

2. What is the positive outcome that will come from your reaction? What's positive for you now and in the future?

3. If your reaction doesn't yield the result you're hoping for, are you prepared for the consequences to follow?

4. How will your response affect your future self?

5. If you react, will you love or hate yourself tomorrow?

Reflecting on my Self Actualization Moment

I needed to have my heart broken for a new light within me to turn on. I needed to be broken to become whole.

I understand any form of love that leads to pain is the worst kind of love and the worst kind of breakup. It is a relationship that I had given everything I had, or so I thought, only to have someone not meet me halfway.

That's why I felt broken into a million pieces and started overthinking why I didn't see the red flags from the beginning. They were there; red flags are always there for those who want to see them.

However, we all make mistakes. Sometimes it's our family members. Sometimes we choose people who are wrong for us. We desperately try to make them right. Because our souls aren't ready, we need to learn yet another lesson. Through the most painful experiences, we learn the most valuable lessons.

Maybe there's no such thing as a mistake, especially if that mistake has taught us something essential about who we are, who we love and what hurts us. And even though we didn't want that love to end, perhaps it was destined to happen.

Maybe we were supposed to get our hearts broken to prepare us for the love of our life, ourselves!

But, for some reason, we couldn't let go. It wasn't because that person was the right one for us but because everything was supposed to happen that way, so we can learn what true love, self-love, really is.

No matter how many times we go back to try to make things work again—they never do because it wasn't meant to be. This acceptance is difficult to comprehend when you're in love but easy to understand once you're back in self-evolution mode.

Healing is not an overnight process. It takes a lot of time, energy, and willpower to do it. It's a constant decision to untie ourselves from the toxicity around us and to become stronger so that disappointments won't get to us. It's the power of knowing that we can love someone, and we can walk away from them with our head held high because we know that we deserve better.

When we do see true love in ourselves, there will be no questions, no drama and no sleepless nights. It will be a love that feels calm and caring. A love that will show us why all our previous relationships failed. Because of everything we went through, every bad relationship or experience was paving the way toward unconditional self-love. And, it will raise us to greatness. Because that's what real self-love does. It makes us whole and brings to the surface the best version of ourselves.

The ME Revealed

As a kid, I didn't have any aspirations. I didn't have big dreams of a big house or a fancy car. My family would ask me, "What would you like to be when you grow up?" In my mind, I thought *anything, but crazy cause that really sucks,* but I couldn't say that out loud. I simply said, "I'm not sure yet." This kept them at bay for a while.

It wasn't until my maternal grandmother introduced me to sewing at the age of twelve that a spark was lit in me! I was finally great at something. Creating unique fashions to wear became my motivation to thrive. I wanted to sew all day and all night.

I couldn't wait for my paternal Uncle Sam to ask me what I aspired to become the next time he picked me up!

Then, the day came. My Uncle Sam and I went out to dinner at a fancy restaurant. Our food was served. On my father's side of the family, we held conversations at the dinner table.

With his stern, yet eager-toned voice, he said, "Yassin, have you decided what you would like to study in college?"

I was ever so excited to tell him; my legs were tapping on the floor. My body was swaying left to right. My smile was infectious; I was giddy. I could hear his laughter as I'm sure I looked quite silly. I proudly burst out and said, "Yes, I want to be a fashion designer!"

I looked at his face; he stopped smiling as I sat there thinking, "Well, that's not what I was expecting at all." He took the napkin and calmly wiped both sides of his mouth. He placed the napkin on the table and said, "There is no money in fashion design, so maybe you should go to the library and research more careers, like business." Just like that, my heart sank; I felt he didn't believe in me, my skills, or my dreams. I did what was expected of me, and off I went to study business.

Don't be disappointed for me; he didn't say where I had to study this major. I'm not one to take the word no and stop there. I've always been that shy little firecracker with a loud inner voice that said, *Really? Watch me! I'll do what is expected, but I'll do it with pizzazz and flare.*

I believed in me, and so did my Mama!

How ironic that I selected a college that also had fashion design as a major as well as being less than a mile away—the Art Institute of Fort Lauderdale. Was it really that ironic? Of course not!

Proudly, I graduated with two degrees: An Associate in Business Management and my bachelor's degree in fashion design that I worked hard to obtain.

I went to school during the day with a toddler in tow, and I worked as the manager at Lerners, earning money to pay for my fashion design classes at night. I dared not tell my family my plans. After all, I already felt like I had failed them time and time again.

I got pregnant at sixteen and was labeled a statistic who would never have a career. Although I graduated twelfth in my class and made the honor roll with an eight-month-old baby, that didn't matter; the shame was already there.

I've had the honor of owning two successful clothing lines: "*Yammiwear*" my children's line and my women's line, "*Let's Journey into Fashion*" which led me to the woman I've become today.

My maternal grandmother, Delia Simmonds, whom I call my "Granny" or "Mama" instilled humbling, spiritual and Godly life values. My paternal grandmother, Ethlyn Lindqvist-Hall, whom I called "Ma" taught me beauty, poise, and grace. My uncle Attorney Samuel H. Hall, Jr. Esq., instilled great work ethics, respecting others as well as gaining respect and introduced me to entrepreneurship at a young age while working in his private law firm. That's where I learned the skills of being my own *BOSS*.

Ma was a founding member of the Business and Professional Women of St. John, United States Virgin Islands in 1965. She was owner and manager of the Hillcrest Guesthouse on St. John in 1966 and named businesswoman of the year. She was also an educator.

I resemble my Grandma Ethlyn Hall RIP

My Mama was an elementary school teacher on St. Thomas. All the women on my mother's side, including my mom, were all teachers. As a child, I told myself I would never become a teacher; it was not appealing to me.

I'm amazed every day how my life, guided by nothing but faith, merged both entrepreneurship and education. Today, I'm a successful entrepreneur educating others about economic development, personal growth, empowerment, and generational wealth by selling products on Amazon, the world's largest online retail store.

As a mental health advocate, I'm educating the educators, teenagers, and families from lived experiences how to notice the signs and symptoms and empowering the first responders to be compassionate toward mental illness.

God turned my purpose into my passion of helping others. He has truly humbled me.

I had the best of both worlds growing up. Being raised biracial—correction, I consider myself a multicultural blended. My lineage, consisting of Caribbean, West Indian, Africa, Denmark, and Spain, has molded me to be an open-minded lover of humanity and completely unbiased about race.

Both of my grandmothers' marvel in their unwavering faith in God.

I lived during the week with my Mama, who became one of my guardians, essentially becoming my mother at the age of fifty-six. I admire her for getting her General Education Diploma in her fifties and graduating college in her sixties after putting all four of her children through college and having only obtained a sixth-grade education herself.

I was even more intrigued by my Mama's strength and unwavering faith in God. At this same time in her life, within just mere months, the following occurrences took place:

Her baby girl's mind deteriorated at the age of thirty-two, diagnosed as a schizophrenic.

With the completion of their brand-new rebuilt home and what should have been their retirement home, it was now filled with both myself, a very angry, confused teenager and my mother, now diagnosed with paranoid schizophrenia. Not to mention, my mother and I slept on the same twin bed despite her attempt to kill me. Yet, my Mama showed no fear.

Four months later, Mama held her husband Eric in her arms as he passed away from complications of having a stroke while parking the car.

This epitome of strength, this less-than-five-foot Godly woman never stopped smiling. She used all this trauma to elevate herself. She enrolled in college and earned her degree in education where she taught children for thirty years.

On February 4, 2019, I had a phone conversation with my Mama in one of our frequent talks, when I tend to draw my strength from her. We discussed that at ninety-two years of age, she to date has had no ailments or even a simple cold, ever. I told her that I appreciated her never giving up on what had to be ultimately the toughest year of her life.

Her response, "Yassin, I didn't do it. God did it. I look back and still don't know how I did it myself. All I can say is I'm grateful that I never wavered in my faith. I feel blessed indeed." I learned the value of putting God first and family second over material things. I look at things acquired as blessings and events that lead to experiences as lessons. I feel blessed to have been born into parallel worlds.

Even today, I'm very humbled about the Hall side of my family as opposed to my open-book life with my Mama. The Hall family are very private, successful people. I've always respected and admired the way they live. I've learned through them the power of owning a peace of mind.

I feel that most won't understand their world. I've invited only five individuals into their house in my lifetime. I've felt that once I've let others into this unique world of mine that their views of me would shift.

Imagine knowing me as this poor child who had blossomed into this down to earth woman, but only to realize—well, damn, she had access to entitlements and the privileged life. The nerve of her! However, my Hall family are not without imperfections. Their world is all about enjoying the finer things in life. They live the grand lifestyle.

To those that have not been exposed to this type of lifestyle, it can lead to feeling inferior about their lives. People tend to judge based on the cover without knowing the actual story. The Hall's earned their lifestyle through their hard work and dedication; it belongs to them.

I was not handed anything. Through my exposure to their finer things in life and their encouragement, I've worked hard for my lifestyle. For that, I'm grateful.

I don't feel I've measured up to the life they would have loved me to have. But I haven't lived my life for their approval; I've lived my life for the approval of God.

I'm joyful of my own lifestyle, however, I know that they are very proud of me. My lifestyle looks amazing from my viewpoint. I may not make reservations at a Five Star A La

Carte restaurant or stay in the penthouse hotel suites, but I have enjoyed having the pleasure of staying and feasting in plenty of them with my Hall family. Although the experiences have been amazing, I personally feel it's a waste of money as this comes from the humbleness instilled from my Mama.

In 2001, four years into my marriage, I traveled with my now ex-husband, Mark Young, to the Virgin Islands for the first time since we started dating in 1996. Prior to our arrival, not once did I discuss my Hall family's way of life. I knew he was not exposed, nor did I feel it should matter. I felt he loved me for me and not for what my family owns.

The family driver and groundskeeper, Curtis, waited for us at the airport. As he drove up the hill, I could see the amusement in Mark's eyes, and he muttered, "Wow! This is really nice," as the electric gates to their house opened.

My boys had been to the house before, so they were all filled with delight to see their Uncle Sam.

As our bags were taken to our living quarters, also known as "the bedrooms." Mark appeared to enjoy the pampering of not having to lift a finger. He was introduced to Maria, the live-in maid. She walked around and showed him where to place our laundry and instructed to ask if her if we needed anything. I remember him asking jokingly, "Is there a butler, too?" All the while, I was thinking that this is why I don't bring others here because they wouldn't understand this lifestyle. To myself and my boys, our driver was our Uncle Curtis who has tremendous pride for his island and enjoyed taking us around educating us about the island's rich beautiful history and sites.

Maria, who washed, cleaned and cooked for us, was like our cousin who lived downstairs. They are our family; we love them.

Every night, we would discuss with Curtis our plans for the next day, so he could take us around the island. After a full day sightseeing or visiting family, we returned to freshly made beds and thoroughly cleaned quarters.

One evening, Mark attempted to iron his shirt and Maria wouldn't let him. The back and forth banter between them tickled me. After a few days of enjoying the pampering, Mark's demeanor changed to disappointment and hurt. He expressed to me that he felt I lied or withheld who I really am.

I didn't feel I lied. I later understood that Mark was working hard to hopefully one day offer us a lifestyle similar to this, less the maid and chauffeur, of course.

Reality set in. He may have felt inadequate of ever surpassing this lifestyle and felt less of a man. I didn't want him to give me a better life. I wanted to simply grow our lives together on what looked and felt good to us.

I knew after this trip that my marriage would be in jeopardy.

From my children's and my viewpoint, the pampering was very welcomed. However, for us, we loved the life we had in Florida more because that was home, and "Home is where our hearts lived with Mark."

In our remaining years of marriage, we chose not to go back to the islands as a couple. When I went to my hometown, I took only the children.

While understanding that you, my readers, may have just swallowed a huge pill of my untold universe, this is my way of being transparent and truthful. I should have proudly shared that my weekend and holiday life were my saving grace and sanctuary home away from the toxic, mental insanity, chaotic, turmoil and bullying of Monday through Friday life. Having a peaceful and carefree life helped me to cope. That's the God's honest truth. An escape to that life gave me hope.

Could you for one moment imagine what my future could have turned out to be without this lifestyle of hope and normalcy?

I have no intention of having a maid or butler, but a chauffeur in Georgia seems like a great dream goal, considering the traffic here!

I, the *mom*, was born on a small island, raised in a small family, and did not have much of a childhood with good memories, such as attending birthday parties, sleepovers or riding bikes in the street with friends. Attending prom or school dances was nonexistent and did impact me, but it didn't define the mother I've become. I wasn't always the mother others see me as—now I'm a put together, well-balanced, compassionate, loving, braggadocious, and precocious mother.

Yes, I've always put my children above everything. But I also can admit I've made a lot of mistakes becoming this mother. Despite my journey into motherhood, the one thing my children can say is that I gave them a childhood of good memories to remember even if it did not resemble those of their peers.

You're probably wondering what I mean by this. Being a single mom with special needs children isn't the norm in today's society. You may see a family with one or two children with special needs. Our awesome God blessed me with four. My eldest son, diagnosed at a young age as bipolar, was also previously diagnosed with Oppositional Defiant Disorder—a disorder in a child marked as defiant and disobedient to authority figures.

My youngest son was diagnosed with autism at the age of three. Autism is a developmental disorder of variable severity that is characterized by difficulty in social interaction and communication and by restricted or repetitive patterns of thought and behavior.

My only daughter had struggled with learning deficiencies until after years of battling with the school system they acknowledged what I had noticed in her. She has the capability of learning, but she requires teaching in a way only she understands. At the age of fourteen, she was formally diagnosed with autism. Also, at the age of fourteen, my middle son showed outward signs of depression.

God had already manifested and exposed me to mental health disorders, and I knew how to get and receive immediate help for my children. They, through me, would have a life of prosperity. I held the power to change the generational outcome that those in my family who suffered from this illness before me could not do.

Being their mom meant I had to navigate through my own weaknesses and strengths to raise them with occasional help from their father, who lives four states away. Yeah, that's a mouthful, and my plate runneth over daily!

All of them had to be disciplined in their own way. Timeout didn't work with the boys, but it did with my daughter. She loved time out! To her, that was her "she space," which ultimately didn't work on my behalf whatsoever. Spanking had zero effect on my eldest. He's one of those children who enjoyed falling the same exact way, every single time, and never learning or accepting the consequences or the lesson. Falling was an accomplishment to him.

Yes, my mind to this day still can't grasp that. Let me give you an example.

Let's say I wanted to teach him that the stove is hot and will burn. "Please don't touch the burners with your hand." Just as I did with my other three children as soon as they were walking around two or three years of age, I would bring them to the stove, turn on the burner and place their hands far enough away so they could feel the warmth. I explained that it was warm, and any closer it is very hot and will burn you badly.

Those three never touched the stove, but this one child, let me tell you what he did! The mother back then screamed at him, *"Boy, what the hell is wrong with you!"* You see, I hadn't learned compassion, nor did I know at eighteen that this was a symptom of an unknown illness. My handsome blessing who saved my life by his mere existence placed his hand directly on the burner, and said, "Ouch, that's hot, Mom," and a minute later placed his other hand on it as well. Now, we were rushing to the emergency room with two burnt hands.

Did that teach him? No! He touched that hot stove a few more times until my grandmother decided to turn off the gas completely. She would walk downstairs every time she needed to cook and turn it back on. This child was just defiant and still is at thirty-one.

My motherly heart aches with deep nested hurt every day for this child. I pray for him the most. He knows he is not mentally well. Yet he refuses to get help. Our hands as his family are tied by the laws of this country that consider him an adult. We can't forcefully make him go for help.

He is a domestic violence abuser toward women I'm unable to protect. As a survivor myself, I feel hurt and helpless that my own child inflicts harm onto unsuspecting women. I've had no other choice but to turn to God and pray to continue to cope. What other options do I have?

The family has had no choice but to disassociate with him because of his severe inappropriate behaviors. He takes little responsibility for his two beautiful children, which in my opinion, is a blessing after being raised watching my mother with her illness.

All I can do is be the best grandma to my grandbabies.

My youngest son loved learning everything, and to some, this would be a great asset. It was, and don't get me wrong, but he needed learning stimulation the entire time his eyes were open. If one of his learning videos ended, then the dropping, kicking tantrum on the floor, blood-curdling screams, running into the walls and the tossing around of whatever was in his grips happened. I made many running dashes to the VCR to quickly start another video for peace of my mind.

Many of you might think he needed a good butt whooping. Let me tell you from my experience that you cannot and should not spank an autistic child. They don't respond well to others being in their personal space as it is. Spanking him was a severe negative reinforcement that drove him inward. It's like looking at a newborn baby chicken walk back into its egg, in its cracked shell and stand inside of the egg trying to put the cracked pieces back together to further isolate itself from the world.

I experienced my daughter taking two to three hours just to write five sentences that were never complete or grammatically correct. For years the words he, she, him, her, I, me, nor it did not come to her mind, and she could not formulate complete verbal sentences with these words. This was my daily life with my wonderful children, and I love them with every ounce of my being. Never dull and full of laughter. Yes, laughter because if I didn't find humor in these kids I would sit in my bathtub and fill it with tears.

Raising them evolved my compassion levels and my acceptance of all humans the world perceives as different or strange.

As soon as my boys turned seventeen, they had a direct flight to my ex-husband to go life. We outwardly joke about our "tag, you're it" comments on social media. By the time my boys started smelling themselves, as we say in the islands, I knew one hundred percent without a doubt that I could not teach these unique male human beings to become a man with what little patience and strength I had left.

So, who is the real Yassin Hall? I'm brilliant at loving other people and giving them hope and inspiration on how to love themselves. Sometimes, my affirmations and spoken words of wisdom reflect onto me. I cringe uncomfortably with every thought in my brain while I'm whispering to myself—*Damn, I needed to hear and practice this as well.*

Just like everyone in this world, I have my moments and I'm not ashamed to admit this is part of being human. For many years, thoughts filled my mind saying that if they really knew me, they wouldn't be complimenting me on my strength. Once they find out how much of a failure I was, how bad I am at meeting my own needs and prioritizing what really matters to me, then they would finally understand why I'm joyful about helping others. Helping others felt better than helping me. This was the period when the opinion of others mattered.

I see the good in others regardless of whether they can see it in themselves. I marvel at how kind, intelligent, giving and loving they are. I see the power they don't see in themselves.

I've always outwardly expressed and understood that no one can save me but myself. I know from experience that telling someone how great they are doesn't matter unless they find a way to believe in themselves.

The more I understand how my self-esteem actually works, the more I love the idea of wanting more of it. Self-esteem is shifting my mindset through affirmations or positive self-talk and taking actions that actually demonstrate that I believe I'm worthy. The hardest question to ask yourself, much less have an answer for...Who are you really?

When naturally self-hatred and doubtful thoughts are the first things that come to your conscious mind, it's a very tough question to find a positive answer for. That is why this chapter was the hardest for me to write. To find the answer would mean I would have to fully identify every single flaw, blemish, hurt, mistake and imperfection to acknowledge, embrace, and develop a plan to take action to accept and openly apologize to myself. Then I could work on being a better version of this woman standing in this dirty grime and cracked mirror staring back at me.

I had to build a better mirror to look through until it became the clearest form of pure glass looking outward at the world and seeing how beautiful it is. I'm blessed to have taken that first step forward with a fresh heart and pure mind.

This took an investment of my time and money doing talk-therapy with a practitioner I trust. With guidance, I'm getting into a regular sleep schedule. I'm also working on how to engage with people I love and with people I've removed from my life. I made the decision not to engage with others if it doesn't help me to love myself. To be better, I am working to spend more time in person with friends I already have and make new friends. I also need to visit friends who live in a different city or state, take risks, and do things I thought I couldn't do. I desire to focus on a growth plan and engage in conversation with others about things I care deeply about.

Most of all, I share with others exactly who I am. All of it. The good, the bad, and the ugly. I smile with joy because this is *me*! This meant that I had to stop treating myself like a child, see myself as an adult, and grow up! In my opinion, self-doubt is your inner self acting like a toddler throwing a tantrum and winning by getting what you want without learning any values or self-discipline. Essentially, I had to tackle doing all the things I've viewed as hard instead of continuously doing the things that were easy.

The woman I've grown into and am still growing into is amazing. I love her.

She is an existence of love, so love will gravitate toward her.

She is energy of goodness.

She is mindful of her thoughts.

She is particular in her choice of words.

She is fluid with her intentions.

She is transparent with her translations.

She is quietly observing everything and everyone.

She will always find a way to do right.

She will align herself with favor.

She will not let fear stand in her way.

She will not be overwhelmed, and even if she does, she will find her happy place to refocus.

She will not be discouraged.
She will not question what feels natural and acknowledge with extreme gratitude the blessings and lessons from God.

She will manifest in her lane while empowering others.

She will be the bold firecracker that she is.

She will stay humble and live in her truth.

She will have gratitude for love.

She will love and cherish God every day.

Chapter One: Single One-Sided Society

So many women choose to stay in toxic relationships because they're afraid of being lonely and criticized by this Single One-Sided Society aka SOSS. Since my inner thoughts prefer to think of SOSS as standing for Sorry Ole Sack of...oh, let me introduce you to my*self.* It's my way to share with you my entire authentic self, and my way of giving you all of my personality.

Society will try to convince you and make you feel like being single is a sickness or a disorder. They are not the deciding factors in owning your power—you are. If you let society decide your happiness, it's possible you and society may end up on the same one-way road to nowhere. Do enjoy that ride; but as for me, I'll take the road less traveled.

As with my last book, I'm sure I'll get scrutinized for opening more of my life. But, again, this will serve as confirmation that I'm doing what God has further led me to do—walk proudly in my truth. Anything that is hard to admit or talk about sets a precedent for owning your power. Some people don't want to hear your truth; they prefer to believe their version of what they think of you, and God forbid you set the record straight with words in a very powerful book.

Every time society or someone tries to disturb my power, I stand in the mirror and repeat the following:

- They can't break me.
- They don't have the power to break fighters.
- You can only scar warriors.
- When those scars heal, so will my power increase.
- Conquerors are built to overcome.

People think if you're a single person, you're miserable and you're a bit lonely. Then there's the other belief that if you're single, what you want more than anything else in the world is to become coupled. However, women are increasingly turning to single living because it is more possible than ever before to live "a full, complete, and meaningful life" as a single person. Every component of a good life is available to you as a single person in a way that has never been true before.

My single personality is nicknamed "the runner" because if it makes me twitch, twinge or sweat, gives me bad vibes, or that feeling of "Oh, no, this is not working for me, " I'll leave with no hesitation. You see, being single is my comfort zone, my sweet Zen, and my happy place.

I'm an only child, and life has forced me to love being and doing things myself. What others call being alone, to me it's being at peace with myself. After overcoming toxic unhealthy relationships, I know I'm worthy of love in whatever way love looks joyful to me.

In some circles, society has labeled me as "The woman who can't keep a man" but from my point of view, it shows I have great strength as a woman. I know exactly what I will or will not allow disturbing my peace of mind or my space. I am a woman who has learned numerous lessons. I'm going to pat myself on my back and continue to elevate loving the woman I'm becoming while encouraging others to do the same.

I've enjoyed being single, and not many can say this and truly mean it. For me, being in a relationship is coming out of my comfort zone, showing that I'm vulnerable, stepping out on faith and trusting that I'm going to gain in some way. I'm either going to gain a long-lasting relationship or learn yet another lesson on this journey.

It sounds easy, but it's truthfully not! It's one of the hardest things for me to do. Trusting and showing I'm vulnerable is terrifying; it ignites my anxiety to the core. I feel detached from myself like someone snatched away my emotional remote control and keep pressing the buttons. A series of confusion takes place because I know that I'm not myself, yet I'm so flustered that my mind and hormones are in warped overdrive. I think the worst of a situation that on a normal day would never have bothered me.

If I want to grow and own more power, I'll have to accept that these feelings are okay. To overcome my anxiety, I have to face the very thing that makes me anxious. In other words, face my fears and tell them I'm not afraid, so bring it on. I'm ready!

I've proven to myself that in every instance of my life, regardless, I'm going to be greater each and every single time. I own so much power that when I love someone again, and things don't work out yet again, I'll cry, hurt and then I'll take time to heal and to love myself more and more. Stay focused on growing from those experiences because God is love. He continues to show me that I'm worthy of someone's unconditional love. Instantly, that terrifying fear goes away. The power is in your belief and unwavering faith.

Singlehood has helped me learn new things about myself and enabled me to please myself and fulfill my desires, wants, and needs. It's provided me with possibilities I never knew existed. It's given me new perspectives on life and showed me what my purpose in life is. Now, from the goodness of my heart, I'm walking the path of helping others in countless ways. It's also enabled me to explore the inner depths of my soul and to devote myself to self-love and self-growth.

I can proudly say I'm not afraid of being single. I'm not afraid to be in a relationship. I'm not afraid of being hurt. I'm not afraid of SOSS. When you have owned your power, fear no longer exists. Therefore, I just live in the moment of being my best self. I'm loving this joyful place of singlehood because it's building a very powerful me. I didn't wake up one day and figure out this strength. I tried on my own, and instead of healing, it increased my anxiety to a level unimaginable — to the point I was suffering from silent anxiety attacks.

Silent anxiety attacks happen when someone who is diagnosed with a panic or anxiety disorder has a panic attack without displaying any outward symptoms. Someone who has had silent panic attacks could have them in public, at home, in the office or virtually anywhere without anyone noticing or realizing that something was wrong.

When my doctor told me that I was having silent anxiety attacks, my first reaction was "Say what, wait…if my attacks are silent, how on earth would I know I'm having one?" After all, duh, it's silent! I was mad because I was in denial. I needed to see my symptoms because how can I control what I can't see? How can I fix invisible? This scared me. It's very real, valid, and frightening for the person experiencing it.

In therapy, I'm learning to find the smallest symptoms in my body as how I'll be able to identify my attacks to control my internal thoughts and emotions happening beyond my control.

I've narrowed down the symptoms that my body shows me:

1.) My right eyelid will not open fully. It becomes a lazy eyelid.

2.) I feel tingling in my arms, legs, fingers, and toes at different intervals.

3.) My goiter swells to a point it wraps itself around my vocal cords, and instantly, in midsentence, I lose my voice.

4.) I can feel depersonalized as if I'm detached from my body. I'm standing in one spot. I'm telling myself to move, run, do anything, and won't move. My brain is in shock of what just happened and has taken a break, however long to process it. When I was told this, I had that moment of *"What you talkin' 'bout Willis, come again?"* Because it's hard to visualize this, it's even harder to explain it as you can see.

5.) I can hear my heartbeat and feel the blood run through it.

One day I had enough of knowing that any day my blood pressure could ultimately spike and stay at stroke levels, and I could die. Imagine knowing your brain, subconsciously on its own, causes your pressure to elevate with minimal symptoms! The only way to know is by taking your blood pressure readings. Now, that's scary. When you are a walking, ticking time bomb, life tends to force you to get help!

I had to hear my own words to others and follow my very own mantra. I'm not okay, and that's okay!

I like to see myself as a strong woman who helps everyone else. Luckily, because of my mother's struggle with mental illness, I'm able to recognize my own needs and reach out, and this year has been no exception. I choose to live mentally well.

I am one hundred percent sure I'm not alone here. I talk to women almost daily who are dealing with some form of anxiety and depression, and they push through it or hide it because they are scared or prideful or even just fully oblivious to the situation. I encourage them to seek help. Seeking help for myself is a no brainer.

The end goal is to own back my power and be healthy. Be in a meaningful, soulful, healthy, unconditional love with the last love of my life. I deserve to be helped sometimes, and there is absolutely nothing wrong with that. That's self-love. Once you have admitted you need help and take action, your first, hardest step is over. Develop a team of supporters who understand your symptoms and can be there emotionally and physically. I'm blessed that my daughter has been to every doctor's appointment and can identify all my medications as well as their dosage. My closest friends are all aware as well.

Since I've shared my vulnerabilities on social media in hopes to empower another woman to own her power, telling the world I'm in therapy to help me to overcome is actually a form of healing that I didn't know I needed. But, God!

I am *extremely* blessed to be my own *boss* and my sisterhood of *bosses* who assist me with my company are so incredibly supportive and helpful. I do understand, though, that you might not be ready to own your power or have the support that you need. In this case, reach out to someone you might not know well, but who may have a living testimony similar to yours. Finding comfort in knowing you're not alone is powerful.

Acknowledging that you are not always required to be perfect and that those expectations we put on ourselves are sometimes keeping us from getting the help we need.

Needing help doesn't mean you have failed; it means you are human. Let's all recognize the beauty of humanity, and, most of all, be your best compassionate self.

In the next chapter, you will learn how I got into my single zone to where I can see myself wanting to walk out proudly, ready for a relationship.

Chapter Two: Single Comfort Zone

To this day, I'm still blurred and confused by the boundaries of the experiences of my past friendships and intimate relationships. I have chosen to Own my Power and to declare clarity and form long-lasting relationships. I'm stepping out of my single comfort zone.

My single comfort zone developed in my childhood. I grew up feeling unsafe, surrounded by chaos, upheaval, and loss. Once I experienced those painful scenarios in previous relationships, it's possible that I over-compensated and guarded my boundaries as well as my routine in order to feel safe.

It's my natural mental way of protecting my mind and emotions. Is it healthy? No.

As a result, I built a protective wall around myself. Now, after living walled-off for so long, I felt severely phobic, uncomfortable and afraid to engage in an authentically intimate, emotional exchange.

I saw my boundaries as a means of survival in a chaotic, untrustworthy world. I made it my routine, and my carefully planned, protected way made it hard for me to allow anyone to enter into my life too deeply.

If I felt a potential partner or friend would alter my life too much, it would feel so uncomfortable that I would force them to push me away. This, however, caused emotional conflict: the desire to protect me from reentering the experiences of my chaotic past versus my awareness of and total comfort with my aloneness, my safe zone, while longing for intimacy and unwavering desire, along with unconditional love.

I became so well-protected that it felt as if I didn't know how to let in any connections. It felt too daunting to accept change, and I was afraid to feel so exposed and vulnerable. For me, emotional involvement feels like an alien language and since I felt unlovable in my past, how could I possibly be lovable now? These are things I told myself until I believed that this is who I had become, so take me as I am or go your way. That was my attitude.

I believed so deeply that letting others in would be at the expense of me damaging or breaking down my beautiful, protective wall. I was forced to recognize this pattern in my life. This self-awareness of my boundaries felt good at the time, but only briefly.

The most bizarre thing is that deep inside, opening myself up to let others into the vulnerable most private parts of my untold truth, intrigued me. I really want to have and desire to feel a positive outcome from letting someone in.

In my life, I have felt comfortable giving another just a taste of me, but not really showing them my true self. Then, bad things happened, or I was left feeling disappointed. I've felt betrayed by those I trusted because they didn't feel I was worthy of a friend or lover enough to not cause me pain. Regardless of the reasons, I allowed my emotions to preempt my ability to engage further and cultivate any intimate, real connection relationships.

Having been exposed to and experienced sexual, physical and emotional abuse is traumatic.

Trauma is insidious and has impacted me more and more over time. My trauma remained under-treated for decades; it affected and polluted my hopes and expectations for any type of future relationships.

My trauma made it seem like my single zone is a safer decision to avoid emotional relationships rather than risking the reenactment of trauma in a future relationship. As daunting as it was, I had to allow myself to seek help and talk about my trauma to dilute the power that trauma held over me, and I'm beginning to open up the possibility of trusting and connecting again. That's how I choose too *own all of my power.*

I intellectually understand the idea of commitment, but for many years, I didn't feel interested in pursuing emotional intimacy at this level. Why? Fear of being hurt.

What is so scary about feeling hurt is that I have tried so hard to avoid it. I've overcome hurt from various effects in life. I've been in a car accident at the age of seven that could have taken my young life, but, yet, I'm not afraid to drive. I've stepped on a nail that had to be surgically removed. Yet, I'm not afraid to buy or hang pictures with nails. I've given birth to not one, but three children and through adoption, we were blessed with my daughter. The experience was the most hurtful, physical pain imaginable. Yet, I wasn't afraid to get pregnant again and again.

What is it about hurt in relationships? One word sums it up: shame. Hurt means that I have to overcome the shame of the emotional hurt I feel for myself and the shameful way others may perceive me. That shame is so intense it can cause me to retreat from others so as not to burden them with it. This experience and way of perceiving myself felt like self-hate, especially directed at this unattractive part of myself.

In the moment of hurt, it's hard to understand how I love myself given the intensity of my emotional needs and trying to imagine that anyone else could love me in this state. To not subject myself to the shame, I try my hardest to avoid relationships altogether.

I felt like my neediness would overwhelm any potential partner and make this person hate me the same way I hated myself, so it seemed simpler to just stay away altogether. This would put me back on track to loving only myself.

Someone told me to my face that they don't feel I even truly understand what a meaningful relationship is. At the time, it was how dare you judge me without knowing me, but I didn't express this out loud. You see, the truth about yourself will always be very visible to others that care about you and your well-being. This very same person boldly called me "selfish" when it comes to relationships, and believe it or not, they still have their teeth, and I didn't punch them in their gut!

On a deeper subconscious level, I may be aware that being attentive to someone else's needs would mean putting my own needs second, which I've already spent a good portion of my life doing, so I retreated to protect myself. After taking care of four kids, I felt selfish that someone needs to take care of my needs for a change.

At this point, it's hard to imagine taking care of someone else's needs. I'm not ashamed to admit I'm afraid to get involved with a partner for fear of losing myself in my partner's needs. That's some serious vulnerability I would have to relinquish. I'm choosing to decide if it's worth breaking the love curse and power through my fears, needs, and inclinations so that I can explore more deeply, intimate relationships with others.

In therapy, I worked towards letting go of shame and anxiety. At times, self-hate that makes me avoid intimate relationships is a win-win. I will find peace and discover how to shift my perspective and make room for intimacy in future relationships.

I will not be ashamed to be hurt in any relationship because I've proven time and time again that I'm a survivor of all hurtful things in life. I've risen every time and can rise victoriously yet again.

Chapter Three: Self-Care and Self-Healing

I consider myself a strong woman; one who helps everyone else. Yet, truthfully, I struggle with recognizing and fulfilling my own self-care needs. I've reached out for help, but not fully accepted it yet. I'll hear the words from my therapist about my mindset, but my stubborn and procrastinating ways stand in my way. I know it's because of two major things.

First, it's hard for me to apply self-care to myself. This is indeed a challenge for me since all my life I've put others' needs and wants first, which leads to short-term, inward fulfillment. I feel good in the moment of helping. Can you relate?

Most people think self-care consists of getting your nails and hair done, getting a facial, makeup makeover, massage, buying something nice for yourself, or having a girls' day or a spa day. While these things feel amazing and worthwhile, that's not all that self-care means. It goes much deeper than that. How do you feel the next day? Still lost and hurt, correct?

Self-care, from my experience, is mental.

It's emotional.

It's healing your mind.

It's conditioning your thoughts. It's the words you speak.

The body language that you project.

It's your posture and how you feel about your reflection in the mirror.

Self-care takes practice and then action in order to heal. It's learning to accept all of life's challenges and coping positively in the midst while maintaining self-control in any situation. Sounds easy, right? It's *the* hardest exam to pass *ever*! It could take months to even years or a lifetime, depending on the power of your mind as well as the amount of trauma you have endured. The end result is happiness regardless of what's happening around you. I lost count on how many times my therapist has told me, "Yassin, you need to make time for self-care." My response, while taking a deep, sorrowful disappointing breath and rolling my eyes, "I know, I'm going to do that."

Second, I have to go back and dig deeper into my past hurt, evaluate how it, every single instance, left me feeling. Feeling that hurt again, talking about that hurt, working through that hurt, and also accepting my contribution, apologizing to myself, and accepting that it's okay for all the wrong or injustice that I have done and that has been done to me was necessary so that I could forgive them and forgive myself. Let go of the hurt and heal.

Many times, my Mama said, "If you want to become better and find joy, the work is up to you," and then I cry. I cry because that means I've got to own my truth about myself, which are the parts of me that are weak and flawed. I push forward because these words from her resonate within me..."To truly find joy is to be completely *free*," and "when you are *free*, no one can ever take your power."

Growing up, my biggest fear was that I would end up just like my mother. And not because I showed any signs, but mostly because the mean bully children would tell me I was just like my mother. "You are crazy." In my community, some looked at me like I was crazy. They treated me like I was crazy. When every day you are told and treated as such, you tend to believe it. How do you tell yourself you are not going end up crazy?

In my world, mental illness was normal, and to me normal was boring, strange, weird, and, most of all, cold-blooded and harsh. Before I made the decision to write *Journey Untold - Twisted Love - My Mother's Struggles with Mental*

Illnesses there was a flame of anger under my skin that ignited me to write that book.

As more people from my Virgin Islands community started surfacing on Facebook and connections were being made, back and forth communications via inbox were taking place. All of my messages, and I'm not exaggerating when I say *all*, started with, "Your mother is the light-skinned woman who walked the street and sat by the waterfront, right? I always wondered what ever happened to you."

These words angered me at the time! I was very ashamed of my mother's illness. Inside was a raging volcano. I wanted to scream and tell them my name is Yassin Hall! It's been over thirty-something years, so why are you still identifying me as my mother's child for God's sake!! Get over that!

My inner Virgin Islander self-thoughts said: *What the hell do you mean by you wondered 'What happened to me'? You never offered an ounce of care, nor did you ever ask how I was doing? You never offered help to my mother! You skinned up your nose up at me, but now you wanna hide behind the phone and wonder about my well-being? Go screw yourself, you assholes!*

Yep, that's how I felt deep inside, honestly. Not because of what they said, but the reason I felt these feelings were because of no other reason than I was so filled with resentment, anger, sadness, madness, hurt, frustration and hatred for the way my young life was, and I never healed.

Of course, I never uttered my true feelings because that would be rude. They would not have deserved that response. It wasn't their fault they didn't know how to be sensitive or compassionate about my situation. That's when it hit me. Educate them and bring them into my life as a youth. Bring the awareness of mental illness to my community. All it takes is one voice, bold and loud enough to ignite change.

I must applaud most of the people I'm connected with from my hometown! I'm super proud to have watched them over the years grow and show compassion for those living with a mental health disorder from my story being told.

There are still some others with so much hatred in their eyes, body language and actions toward me because of reasons unbeknownst to me. One person, in particular, texted me in 2018, "Wish you would just die," and even others are waiting, tapping their feet for my "crazy" to show its raging head just so they can have the satisfaction of saying, "I told you that bitch is crazy." I've seen the screenshots of those text messages and never gave them my energy with a response.

The only reason I'm even mentioning it now is because of my *Journey Untold*, and I'm the one telling it from my viewpoint. This is the journey I travel daily.

To those I pray for, I hope they too seek professional help. God, please put your healing hands on them, show them how to love others, but, more importantly, themselves. Amen. I can't stop their negativity; that's not my job. I've chosen to hit that wonderful key named "*block*." I *own* the *power* to only let the positivity shine through in my happy little world where they don't exist.

I'm focused on elevating more as a woman and in my faith. I must confess, I didn't randomly wake up and tell myself, *Yas, get up and get help.* My life had to hit rock bottom physically and emotionally, unfortunately.

The signs of me needing help showed up a long time ago, but no one listened, and services weren't available. I remember very clearly at the age of fourteen saying out loud, "If I was no longer around, everything would be better off." I was told to "Get over it." What else was I supposed to do but suppress it and "Move on with it" like a piece of thirty-year-old raggedy luggage with no wheels dragging on the floor behind me?

I am one hundred percent sure that I am not alone here. So many of us women are dealing with some form of anxiety and depression daily, and they push through it or hide it because we are scared or prideful or even just fully oblivious to the situation. I am here to tell you, *it's okay to not be okay.* It's okay to need help.

Admitting it to yourself is the first step. This was probably the worst part for me. I have built my own personal identity on being a strong, independent woman who takes care of everything solo. I should be able to handle this on my own, right? *Wrong.* We deserve to not just barely make it through every day. We deserve to be the ones who are helped sometimes, and there is absolutely nothing wrong with that.

In between 2006 and 2009, what could go wrong happened. Divorced, broke, hungry, homeless and helpless with four children. The "I'm losing myself" moment happened for me when eldest son was shot in the back five times. Afterward, I called the police, put him out and left him on the front lawn still wrapped in bandages, sitting in a wheelchair only a month into his recovery.

Ask for help!

The second worst part for me was admitting that I was struggling. After watching my son's friends pick him up that day in 2009, from the window crying, I finally picked up the phone and called a therapist.

I know this sounds like I'm cold-blooded, but I'm not. I just reached my "had enough" stage with his illness, and I had to look at my three younger children and do right for them. He was an adult. You see, there is a testimony for every action taken. This is mine. Being a parent or caregiver of someone living with a mental health disorder can drain you emotionally. My son was diagnosed with multiple personalities as well as bipolar borderline schizophrenia.

For most of his life, the family has spent thousands of dollars on care, rehab, bail, legal defense, therapy, etc. None of it stopped his stealing, drug use, con-artist ways, manipulation, lies, violent and severe lows. His behavior worsened after he was shot. Instead of the shooting humbling him and increasing his faith in God, in his mind he became invincible and acted as such with severe reckless behaviors. He resided in Florida months before his shooting. He called me one day crying and said that he couldn't make it in the states, he was being evicted and he was moving back to St. Thomas.

My heart sank that year as the Virgin Islands had a high number of homicides with most being young men in their twenties losing their lives. According to the crime data, fifty-six homicides in the U.S. Virgin Islands in 2009, up from forty killings in 2008 and forty-five in 2007. With a population of about 110,000, the U.S. Virgin Islands had a homicide rate in 2009 that was about ten times the USA's national average of five killings per 100,000 people.

I begged him not to go, but he went anyway. We got into an argument, and I told him if he ends up dead, I'll bury him in a garbage bag, and I'm not coming to his funeral. I didn't mean it at the moment. I wanted to scare him by saying things and not thinking that I'd regret hoping he would stay in Florida.

I know my child; he is a follower of bad company, not a leader. He will do anything to fit in. My gut knew he would end up in a gang. I felt hopeless and afraid that I'd lose my son. Sure enough, he did join a gang and it was the leader of the gang who put a hit on my son. He was the thirteenth victim and one of the few who survived that year.

He was airlifted to the hospital in Orlando; I was told he arrived with nothing, no clothes or shoes. I could barely afford food, and now I had to take care of this grown adult who refused to take his medication. As an adult, I couldn't force him, and he refused psychological evaluations and free mental health care to cope with being a victim of gun violence. Saying I was stressed out was an understatement. With no job, I relocated to Orlando to be by his side. I had no money, barely any food, and one more mouth to feed.

A friend of mine knew my situation and sent my son three large boxes of new clothes and shoes. Instead of saying thank you, this child said, "I am not wearing any of these. They are not my style, and my friend should have asked him what he liked." I was fuming mad at the level of total ungratefulness!

Within that month, he tormented and threatened harm to my younger boys and my daughter. My children were afraid to leave their rooms. Tensions were high in our house. Barely able to afford bills and food, I told him to please conserve power, turn off the lights and stop leaving the TV on all day and night.

This defiant child refused, so I did what I had to do and turned the power off at the breaker for the entire house.

This made him raging mad, and he decided to walk around the house with his walker and threatened to hit all of us with it. I guarded my kids behind me against the kitchen counter. He would have to hit me, but he was not going to hit them, not as long as I was alive. That's when I called the cops. This made him even more irate. He started smashing dishes, threw all the TVs on the floor, ripped pictures off the walls and launched them at us while cursing. My children were crying and screaming for him to stop. I, however, kept calm and prayed. I never showed fear. I knew I could take him down, but my kids had seen enough, and I had to protect my younger children.

The police came rather quickly and agreed with me. They ordered him to leave the house. The police didn't leave until his friends drove off with him in the car. Standing in self-hatred, feeling horrible, I asked myself, "How does a mother put her own child in this condition out of the house?" Have I no compassion? I'm supposed to love my child unconditionally. The guilt of a mother is real. I couldn't deal with this level of guilt on my own.

I looked at my three other children, scared and crying in my arms, telling me all the horrible things he had done. Hearing all of this for the first time, I said to them, "I had no idea." That's when I realized that we all needed help, not just me.

Painful love is the worst kind of love.

My children needed me to become healed and whole. Therapy always reassured me that I'm not required to be perfect, and those expectations that I put on myself were keeping me from getting the help we needed. Needing help doesn't mean I failed as a mother; it meant I'm human. That meant what I did was the right thing. Things could have gotten worse that day to all of us if I didn't put my eldest son out.

Life isn't just about being happy and maintaining that happiness to ultimately feeling joyful...It's not about how you feel second-to-second in any situation. It's about what you're making of your life and whether you can find a deep pride in who you are and what you've been given.

This is the same concept to apply for failed relationships. Lord knows I've had my share of those as well. In the next chapters, I'm opening my vulnerability to a level like no other for me. Exposing my truths, pain, and triumphs. I'm focusing on the lessons I've taken away in each one as they all have taught me so much about myself.

In order to live a joyful life. You must release all your anger. One of the first steps to releasing anger is to understand the power behind the emotion. Anger causes us to be smaller than we want to be. To not stand in our glory and greatness causes us to contract and robs us of feeling love and peace of mind.

I love the woman I'm becoming more and more every day.

One of the greatest lessons I've taken away from being in relationships that were just not meant for me is that every man wants that good woman until that good woman requires that man to be a good man. That's when it all unravels for me.

Chapter Four: The Absent Father

Victor Arthur Emmanuel Hall, an entrepreneur, and my father, to whom I'm his only child. Victor was born in New York on February 15, 1950 and departed this life on March 2011. He was best known as the owner of the Kite, a legendary Northshore bar that operated at Peter Bay, St. John in the 1980s.

In 1986, the infamous "Kite" showcased ABC's Good Morning America jamming his song "2000 Miles from Reality" with Paul Shafer and NBC's David Letterman Show and other musicians from around the world. Victor wore many hats; he was a musician, a fisherman, and an engineer. You name it, and Victor could fix it when it came to electronics.

He was known as the "Medicine Man" for his passion for herbal bush teas, which could cure just about any illness, he would say.

May 25, 1985

Washington Post Article

In 1954, Laurence Rockefeller took one look at St. John, an island with only twenty-four hundred inhabitants, smaller than Manhattan, and promptly bought half of it.

"Paradise," he said when he saw Caneel Bay and decided to keep it that way. He bought more than five thousand acres, donated it to the National Park Service, and retained 170 acres to build an understated, but elegant resort at Caneel Bay. Now more than two-thirds of the island is under park protection.

Leaving Caneel Bay Plantation and moving along on the shoreline road, which overlooks some of the most famous coral reef beaches in the world, the rental jeeps and island taxis plunge pell-mell around the curves, and 35mph feels like seventy (it's think left, drive left).

You can't resist stopping at The Kite, a little open-air shack, clinging to a cliff above the water where Victor Hall, a local musician, fed and entertained the young and adventurous and rented camping space on Peter Bay. Potatoes are peeled for French fries while you watch. And the popular morning drink is Baileys Irish Cream and Kahlua.

May 26, 1989

Los Angeles Times wrote:

"The Kite is my favorite hangout on St. John. It's a clean roadside shack with a tiny bar and a deck that hangs above

a pair of turquoise bays and powder-white beaches. At The Kite, a laid-back, personable St. Johnian named Victor Hall serves his delicious version of the Pina Colada and strums a 12-string guitar to the accompaniment of an electronic rhythm box as he sings.

Boats sail by, and while aboard, sailors do their fancy stuff in Cinnamon Bay below. And suddenly your part of Hall's band, playing whatever, you grab from behind the bar— from drums and congas to tambourines and maracas."

Hue of Fire

The sun sets in a hue of fire. As you look to the horizon, you can see a chain of emerald cays ringed with white sand set in an active passage between the British Virgin Islands and the U.S. Virgins.

Although Hall opened The Kite when the mood struck him, a great time to visit was in the afternoon after a session on the beach.

The light-green shack that housed The Kite was on Northshore Road between Cinnamon Bay and the famous Trunk Bay in Virgin Islands National Park.

In 1989, Hurricane Hugo caused significant damage to the Virgin Islands. In recovery from the aftermath, Victor used a generator that caught fire. He received second and third degree burns to over half his body. The Kite burned to the ground.

Victor healed himself with herbs, and thus became known as the "medicine man."

I wish I could tell you that I knew him as well as others did. However, I'm comforted by the kind words expressed to me about the man they knew.

Society interprets fathers that are not active in their children's lives as "bad fathers." In my view, a bad person is someone who has no regard for your well-being and applies hurt. It can be emotional, mental, or physical hurt.

I don't view him as a "bad father," although the things he said to me hurt. I understand that he cared enough for me enough to know that he wouldn't be the best choice to raise me. He was my absent father. I saw a man who was focused only on his own inner happiness and surrounded by his first love, music, and his friends.

He lived on the sister island to where I lived on St. Thomas. Just a twenty-minute boat ride and a twenty-five-minute taxi ride into Charlotte Amalie, the capital. This does not sound far, does it? Less than an hour away! Yet, I did not physically see my father's face until I was twelve years old.

As a child, I felt like my father could have spared one hour of his time to spend with me. Was I that much of a disgrace to him? This thought has crossed my mind many times. I would speak to him over the phone when my grandmother would call him to discipline me. I don't recall a single time he called just to say "hi, I love you," and to tell me that he was proud of me.

From my experience, he was unknowingly an emotional abuser to me. His words hurt me. He made promises only to continuously break them. I wanted so badly to believe each time that he would keep his word and come over to see me.

A week or so after my mother had her nervous breakdown, I laid eyes on my father for the very first time. I was sitting on the stand in the courtroom on St. Thomas answering the judge's question regarding my mother's behavior. This hearing took place to revoke my mother's parental rights, and the judge would make his decision as to who would become my legal guardians.

The judge asked me to explain what happened the day my mother threatened my life. As I was just trying to find the strength to tearfully explain, a man jumped up screaming at me from the chairs behind my mother's public attorney's desk. "She is lying! She did this to her mother!"

There I was trying to fight my fears, trust the judge, and feel safe to even admit that, yes, my mother had a problem and to please help her. I found my brave voice and had the chance to discuss my pain to someone about the tragic day that forever changed my life. Just as I was ready to overcome the shame and guilt inside me, this loud man scared me into silence. I refused to discuss with anyone about what happened that day until I wrote *Journey Untold* some thirty-three years later.

The judge banged his gavel and yelled, "Order in the Court! " just like in the movies. He recessed the hearing and indicated that afterward that we would meet in his private chambers. I remember my Ma wrapping her arms around me, wiping my tears and rubbing my back, and telling me that everything was going to be okay. I asked her, "Was that my father?" She responded in a very sorrowful yet disappointed tone, "Yes."

Inside I was screaming, *why would he say I'm lying*? I just could not understand! He was not there! He has never been there to see what we saw every day. *Why would he embarrass me like this? Why would my father hurt me, especially at this time? Could he not see I was already hurting and dying inside?*

After the break, in a room no more than ten feet on each side, we sat at an oval mahogany table. The judge was at the head of the table. My Ma was on his right side, and I was next to her. My aunt, my father's sister, was next to me. My father sat near the end of the table. Next to him, his other sister. My Uncle Sam sat just to the left of the judge.

The judge began the hearing. He turned to my father and informed him that because he was my father, I was his legal responsibility. What my father said next was the most hurtful thing I'd heard. He said, "I have no interest in taking care of her. I want nothing to do with her. I'm not in any position to take care of her."

Everyone gasped with shock and shame, but not me, I broke down in uncontrollable tears. My Uncle Sam was so angry that he slammed his hands on the table and said, "I will take care of her."

A social worker removed me from the judge's chambers. I was emotionally devastated. In less than a month, emotionally and mentally, I felt I lost both parents who from my view, hated me. And, I couldn't understand the why for any of it.

If your own parents don't want you, who on earth will? That's how I felt. I can't recall how long I remained outside. I do, however, remember going back into the judge's chambers. This time, only my uncle and my ma were at the table. The judge apologized to me for what I had to endure. He awarded joint guardianship to my ma and Uncle Sam.

I lived with so much anger toward my mother and my father. I did not speak to nor see my father for many years after this incident.

The next time I heard my father's voice happened over the phone when his sisters called him to inform him that I was pregnant. When they handed me the phone, he called me a bitch, whore, and a slut, without knowing that a man invaded my body and took my virginity without my approval.

At this point, I was so deeply emotionally damaged, yet numb to his words. There was no further damage his words could do. I hated my very existence. Subconsciously, I had to emotionally detach from his hurtful words for my own sanity.

I heard from my father in my adult years via a fifteen-page email. It included more name-calling, more insults, and he told me that I was a snake in the grass. He reacted this way because I chose to have my uncle walk me down the aisle on my wedding day. In his mind, he felt betrayed and he was hurt.

After my mother passed away, a friend insisted I take this opportunity to visit my father and tell him exactly how I felt. However, I was scared to confront him as I wasn't sure if I could face him and not run my fists down his throat to erase all the emotional trauma, inflicted on me over my lifetime. He was my father, and I had so many unanswered questions.

As his child, I experienced emotional hurt so often I believed that what happened to me was normal, and there was something wrong with me. When someone is not given what they need for healthy growth, it becomes a part of who they are. This type of abuse gave me an overdeveloped sense of guilt and shame over things I didn't do—things that were out of my control. I felt responsible for the failed relationship with both my parents. I took the heat for their bad behavior. It was my fault that they couldn't offer me love or understanding.

I know this all sounds stupid, but these have been my internal replays for a long time. In many ways, I had to learn in therapy how much they were engraved into my subconscious. It affected virtually every choice I made in life. It was time to stop this curse that plagued my life.

I overcame that fear and took my daughter with me. This was the first time he would lay eyes on any of his grandchildren. Filled with resentment, it was quite awkward for me to stand in front of him. I knew in my heart the air finally needed to clear and to say what I've always wanted to tell him to his face.

He started to reminisce on moments he shared at "The Kite." He told my daughter that he was on Good Morning America.

It was in that moment I hit my "enough" level, and the words flew out of my mouth. I told him I never wanted to hear that story again, and that the only reason I was there was to find out why he chose to not be a father to me.

He explained that "he was not able to find a wife to take care of me."

It was in that moment I wondered whether he could also possibly have some sort of mental health disorder. None of what he said made any sense to me, and I told him that. I told him I needed a father and not another woman to raise me. Why could he not have done that one thing?

He honestly answered by saying, "I didn't know how," but that was not the answer that I wanted to hear. At that moment, I was not sure how to feel. Do I give him respect for his honesty or dislike him more for being totally honest?

I changed the subject to the relationship he had with my mother. He said he had always loved her.

I told him about the day my mother wanted to end my life. Every time he tried to silence me, I said, "No, you are going to listen to me. At the very least, you owe me this much!" I felt so empowered, and I had no idea where that feeling of strength came from. He grabbed a chair and calmly took a seat.

What he said to me after giving me the chance to finally tell him exactly what happened, took me by surprise. He jumped up and said, "When your mother left me that morning, she was fine!" Total confusion haunted my soul as I had no idea where my mother had gone that life-changing morning. I dug deeper. I wanted to know why my mother was on St. John to see him on that very day. I could feel the anger inside seeping into my spirit.

According to my father, both of them confronted his mother. He told Ma that he was going to marry my mother, and there was nothing else she could do to stop it. He angrily stated that Ma refused to approve of them being married. That she threatened to disown him and write him out of her will, leaving him nothing.

With this off-the-wall statement, my life, just like that, was finally beginning to make sense. I asked him, "What did you decide?"

This man, with whom I share the same DNA, told my mother to leave as he needed the land.

I felt every single emotion towards him—anger, frustration, hatred, sadness, and madness. Oddly, at that moment, I understood why my mother showed up to my Mama's house so unlike herself and so angry. She was not angry with me after all. She was angry with him. Is it possible that she needed to release me from his hurt, and ending my life was her solution?

I know this sounds cynical, but I now wonder is it possible that my mother was not trying to kill me? In her mind, she was trying to save me. *Wow!* I needed to process everything because this new perspective changed the entire outlook, I had of myself. After forty years of feeling that I was to blame, I was not the blame at all.

We paused, and I took pictures with him and my daughter. I respectfully declined to take any with him. Today, had I known that day would be the last time I would see him alive, I would have taken our first picture together.

By 2010, Ma had already decided and gifted her land to her children, except my father. She gave me over an acre of land with a beautiful house. My father used that moment to tell me that I should have refused the gift and given it to him because rightfully it was due to him.

I kindly told my father:

1. You have never done anything for me.
2. You have given me nothing but empty broken promises.
3. You have insulted my name several times.
4. I'm just learning that you pushed my mother to her "enough" stage that in turn caused me to have a confused and turbulent youth.

No way on God's green planet was I going to offer you anything!

I'm not sure if he truly comprehended what I said as he responded by asking me if I knew if his mother left him anything in her will. That was it for me; it was going nowhere. We said our goodbyes.

My daughter and I took the ferry back to St. Thomas. During that twenty minutes ride, I felt calm throughout my body. I was slowly coming to peace with myself. The truth was beginning to set me free.

When we returned to Florida, and out of the blue and the goodness of my heart, I sent my father some money. That was my last communication with him.

Victor Went Home

I received an email from his sister. It said, "Victor died."

At first read, I thought how cold of a message. My brother died and no other information.

She lived a minute from the hospital and was able to identify the body, but she refused to go. My uncle, who lives over an hour away, went to the hospital and confirmed it was my father.

Just like that, in a one-year span, I lost both parents. Reality set in, and I selfishly thought once again that they left me all alone and hurt.

I later found out my father laid in his living dwelling for two days. He died alone from a heart attack.

I felt so sad. In life, he was so alone and died that way as well.

His going home celebration...

Let me say that this was the ultimate, most stressful event of my entire life. I'm his only next of kin. We did not have a relationship. Ma felt that as he was her son, everything should be conducted the way she wanted.

My two aunts (his sisters) were on the internet saying all these wonderful things about him. Yet, they disowned him for many years and never offered him bread or said hello as they passed him on the street. Set of two-faced, hypocritical...it's not even worth mentioning what they are. Let the irrelevant stay irrelevant.

I feel they wanted to pacify their own guilt by doing something nice for him and to put up a false facade in front of the community, friends, and family.

Guess who had the last and final say? Me. It was my decision to give my father the goodbye that he would have wanted. Since I did not know him well, I contacted his friends, those who knew the wonderful side of him. Together with my Uncle Sam and we gave my father a musical tribute in the church where all his music buddies played their favorite tunes with him over the years. We all danced and celebrated Victor Hall that day. It was awesome to see how much he was loved and that he brought joy to others through his first love, music. That warmed my heart.

What was truly sad, totally embarrassing and just insulting was that none of his sisters showed up to either of the two funerals held nor did they bring his mother to say goodbye to her child. The distance was not the reason as they could have walked five minutes down the hill.

I know what you're thinking about how could anyone be so cold and heartless, right? I thought so too. As the saying goes, karma is real! God don't like ugly, and he never sleeps.

After the funeral, my hurt and anger started to turn into compassion for my father. I understand now that he loved me enough to know I deserved better. He was right. Still, it lingered in me whether my father had a mental health disorder. In my gut, that was the missing piece of the puzzle toward me loving him for who he was and letting go of the hurtful emotions.

On my last days on the island, my Uncle Sam and I attempted to find where he was staying all these years, so we could clean his belongings. What we saw when we arrived left us both speechless. We both stood at the front entrance, less the door. The door was gone, not stolen. It was never there to begin with. The windows and bathroom were also missing.

To better describe the structure, it was a small cottage house that construction had begun on, but the house was never finished. He lived in this for God knows how many years. We stood there in utter shock. I felt like I was going to throw up. My uncle grabbed my hand for comfort. We both could not comprehend what we were seeing. My father was a hoarder and lived in filth with animal and insect feces around him. Yet, nobody in the family knew. At that moment, as his daughter, I felt so bad. As much as I was struggling with my own life, my father lived in a worse way. How awful. Barely anything was salvageable. I found some homemade afro music picks, but that's about it. The hazmat crew had to get rid of the rest.

His friends later told me that he was ashamed and never wanted me to know how he lived.

Here I stood with the instant realization that I had two parents struggling with mental illnesses, and they never received help. Saying I'm truly a blessed child of God is an understatement. Life in its own time has a way of opening your eyes, revealing your truth that you were exactly where you were meant to be.

Chapter Five: Innocence Stolen

Close your eyes for a moment and imagine if you would a childhood never experienced.

During my elementary school days, my Mama would cook breakfast for us and make sure I was dressed for school. My mother would pick me up, hop on the bus, and walk me to the door of my classroom. At lunchtime, the school allowed my mother to sit and have lunch with me. In my own way of coping, I would tell myself I'm so much more loved than the other kids whose parents did not come to eat lunch with them.

After school and as soon as the classroom door opened, there my mom stood waiting for me. Not with a smile or a hug, just a very serious face. She would take my hand, and we spent the afternoon sitting on the waterfront, singing and enjoying the water and watching the sunset. My mother would take me back to my Mama. Mama would have dinner ready and help me with my homework as my mom went to her apartment on the island somewhere.

Once I started middle school, my mom was inward deep with sadness, if that was even possible. Her eyes were blank. Her body language was motionless. I rarely saw her except when I walked by the bench on the waterfront where she would sit for hours. There she sat, laughing as she talked to herself. The mother I knew had left; this new person existed.

I was happy she was laughing after seeing her sad all the time, but at the same time, I wanted her to share her laughter with me in my dark, what felt loveless, cold, hurtful world, but she never did. She had her nervous breakdown, a term that I will never understand but I digress to say she lived in a separate world. In her new world, I didn't exist, and she was free, totally free of any of life's responsibilities.

Outside of her world, it was my Mama and my grandfather Eric, briefly before he passed away, painfully watching her mind fade away.

Mama and my life were robotic. We'd wake up and pray, pray and then eat, go to school, come home and get ready for church, pray over dinner and then complete homework Monday through Friday.

On the weekends, I had more exposure but not much outside of the family interaction. It consisted of backyard barbeques, going to the beach and movies, and playing video games with my cousin-in-law Stephen, the son of my uncle's wife at that time.

To say that I was sheltered is putting it mildly.

At the age of sixteen, I was still this innocent virgin, living on an island and naive about the dangers of those with evil intentions. I'd never been exposed to danger to know what it would look like even if it did present itself. Just a week after my birthday, one of my cousins asked me to go with her to a dance at the high school in the countryside. I asked my Mama if I could go. After many questions and debates, she told me yes, but that I had to be back home by 9 p.m. She asked me who was driving. I lied and told her my cousin's mom will take us.

I knew from the beginning that the driver of the car was my cousin's boyfriend's friend. I did lie to Mama because I knew it was wrong. I didn't think something would happen to me. I knew she would not have approved of me riding in a car with someone she didn't know.

My Mama didn't trust any boys or men around me. I knew if I told her a man I barely knew was driving, then she most definitely would say no. I wanted to experience a dance for the first time in my life. I wanted to just be a normal teenager for a moment as it was a teen dance.

My cousin and I wore matching outfits. A white sweater with Mickey and Minnie Mouse with a red knitted straight skirt down to our knees. We all met in the garden in town and drove to the countryside of the island. We made a stop in front of my cousin's house. My cousin and her boyfriend went into the house.

I was sitting in the front seat of his car listening to the blaring music. I did not say anything to the driver. I just sat there listening. Moments went by, and I began wondering what was taking them so long.

The driver asked me if I was thirsty, and I said yes. We proceeded to drive. At that time, I was not familiar with the countryside. I grew up in town, so of course, I didn't know where anything was nor where I was going. I noticed that we were passing homes and then there were just trees around us. He made a right turn up a steep dirt hill.

At this point, I asked him, "Did they put a store in the bushes? "

He didn't say anything. He just looked at me, smiled, and kept driving up this dark dirt road.

I did not feel scared. As I said, I had no idea what danger was. I felt curious as to why would they build a store so far from everything.

The car stopped. I was scared now! He turned off the car with the music still playing. Then, hurled his body onto mine in the passenger's seat. I was yelling for him to get off of me. He placed his lips on mine. I turned my head left and right to avoid his kisses.

I scratched, punched, and kicked my legs back and forth, and up and down.

In my young, naive mind, we were fighting, and he was trying to beat me up. One thing I knew how to do was to fight, but he had the upper hand. There was not much space in the front seat to give him a good beat down.

He grabbed both of my tiny wrists with one hand, and I, at that moment, did not know where his other hand went. My hands were tightly gripped, but my legs kept kicking hard.

He grunted with disappointment. He was mad and let my hand go while pushing them away. He pushed my body so hard that my head hit the window. All this time, I was thinking, "Why, God? Why would this man bring me all the way up here just to fight me?" He was angry, and the music was still playing. My body language was upset because I lost the fight. This man had beaten me up. What for? I don't know.

Feeling bad for not winning this fight, I stayed calm. He reversed the car and drove back to my cousin's house. They were waiting outside. I got out of the front seat and moved to the back. My cousin sat next to me and asked me what was wrong. Out of fear, I told her nothing was wrong.

We went to the dance, and I stood in the corner the entire time. I just wanted to go home and cry because I lost a fight. That's all I knew happened to me.

In hindsight, I know now that my cousin and her boyfriend went into the house to have sex and left me outside. Some people would hold grudges or resentment, but I never did. It was not her fault that my cousin's boyfriend's friend did what he did. You see, I did not know the word "rape" existed. I could not describe what happened besides what it felt like to me. There was no penetration that I was aware of. No liquid on my clothing.

In my young mind, I came to the conclusion that he tried to kiss me and since I refused, he started to beat me up. He didn't punch back or hit me in the face. I didn't leave bloodied or penetrated, but he did have scratches. My wrists were red and bruised from him holding them so tightly. A few days later, my legs had black and blue marks.

I wanted to tell someone what he had done, but who could I tell and exactly what could I say? I allowed this man I barely knew to take me in his car alone to a store that didn't exist. Instead, he took me up a dark, dirt road and picked a fight with me because I would not kiss him.

We already had one crazy person in our house. No room for two crazies. I said nothing.

Months went by, and my stomach was getting bigger. My Mama asked me, "When did I last do number two?" I told her I couldn't remember. She made me some tea, so I could do number two. My stomach was still big.

She made an appointment to see Dr. Calendar. He was asking me questions about my period. My Mama told him that I had one briefly back in December, but I thought I cut myself shaving for the first time. They both chuckled. I did too; it was the way they said it. Plus, I was embarrassed.

He asked if I had sex. I looked at my Mama as if to ask, "What's sex?" I was not about to say the word "sex" to my Christian grandmother. She didn't care about us being in the public as she would still slap me. I knew better.

She responded, "No, she did not have sex."

He asked her if he could examine me, and she approved.

I was lying on the table, knees up in a stirrup, feeling immensely uncomfortable. He put on gloves, and I was looking scared at his ten-foot-sized -looking long fingers. He proceeded to tell me it might feel uncomfortable, and I'd feel some pain.

Oh my gosh, some pain? That was more than pain!!! I gave off a hurling scream, and he pulled his hand out quickly.

He looked puzzled. My granny asked, "What's wrong and is she pregnant?"

The doctor said, "Yes, but medically speaking, she is still a virgin. Her hymen is still in tack, and I will have to break it to give her a full evaluation."

I laid there thinking, "What are they talking about. What's a hymen? Pregnant? What's that? Of course, I'm a virgin. Duh, I was born in the Virgin Islands." Nothing made sense to me.

But I dared not ask any questions. Have you heard the saying "Fear God"? Well, I feared my grandmother more. She was not abusive, just a very stern Caribbean woman. I have the utmost respect for her and her Christian values.

Dr. Calendar tells me I had to bear the pain and called in a nurse. I was crying and screaming.

Yeah, what a great way to break your virginity for the first time, and how memorable.

While lying through all this, I was thinking that a man four years older than me decided it was his place to take my innocence without my consent. From that, my first child was conceived.

When I turned sixteen, I felt life would be easier on my entire family had I not been born or alive. I had plans to jump over the waterfront and make everyone happier as I believed that my mom's mind would return from schizophrenia if I just disappeared. I never developed the courage to pursue my thoughts and five months later, the doctor said, "She is pregnant."

Even on the drive back home, in my young mind, I had no clue what anything the doctor said meant exactly. It wasn't until my grandmother asked me "Who is the child's father" that it dawned on me that being pregnant meant carrying a child inside. To say the least, it was definitely a quick reality check. It was at that moment I realized God had given me my reason to live, my very first blessing in what had been a very dark sixteen years of my existence.

A month later, my paternal aunts decided to take me on a trip to Orlando, Florida for what I believed was a trip to Disney World, the land where dreams come true. Once we arrived, they drove me to a doctor's office. I kept hearing the word abortion, but again, I was only sixteen and naïve. I just figured that was a grown person's word that I was supposed to know. The doctor said they needed my parent's consent. Well, I knew they were not going to get that consent from my mentally ill mom nor my Christian grandmother, so the only other option, call my nonexistent father, their brother.

Let's just say their plan foiled as my father had no clue if I was alive or dead, much less pregnant, and, boy, he was fuming mad at all of us. He called me a bitch and a whore. In my mind, as usual, I thought, whatever, you don't even know me. Stay on your little island and leave me the hell alone, cause you're so great at not being there.

I had a blast on vacation at Disney World with my cousins and two pouting aunts in tow.

Once I returned on the island, my family, at this point, wasn't speaking to me. For the rest of my pregnancy, I was rather lonely. I felt like I shamed them, although someone else did this to me.

I didn't press charges as I did not have a strong case. There was no such thing as testing DNA back then, and medically I was still a virgin.

Inside, I knew I was the victim but to the locals, I was the problem and it was my fault. I was in my senior year in high school, and the kids would call me such cruel names that in no way depicted who I was. How could I explain to other sixteen-year old's that someone took my innocence and that they should believe I was not promiscuous?

At two o'clock in the morning on October fifth, my contractions started. My grandmother rolled out of bed and dropped me off under the drive-thru tarmac of the emergency room. She told me, "Get out here. Call me when the baby is born because I have to go to work." I remember thinking, but wouldn't dare utter this to her, "Wait, you're not coming in and helping me through this? I'm only sixteen!" How blasted cold and inhumane. To understand my grandmother, think of the old folks' saying..."A hard head makes for a soft behind"... in her mind, I didn't heed her warnings of dangerous people in the world, basically implying that was the consequences of my actions and the price I had to pay.

After the birth of my son, I woke in my hospital room with a couple sitting in the corner. Moments later, my grandmother walked in and said, "They are here to take the baby." It was at this time my sixteen-year-old mouth had something to say and respect for my elders went out the window. I mean, what gave her the right to go to that extreme step of actually finding a family and bringing them in my room? I remember thinking *if the trauma of giving birth by myself was not enough, that right there was the icing on the cake.*

Needless to say, my voice was heard; I took a stand for what was right for me, and my first blessing came home with me. That blessing became my everything; the air that I breathed. From a situation that could have scared me for life emotionally, God blessed me with that beautiful child of mine.

You're probably wondering what happened to his father. On the drive going to one of my doctor's visits, I saw him walking along the road and my Mama was driving.

I said, "Mama, do you want to know who the baby's father is? That's him walking."

This lady pulled off the road and screamed at him, "Young man, come here! "Do you know my granddaughter?"

He rested his arms on the car door, then placed his head into the window to look at me. He said, "Yes, she wanted to be my girlfriend but found out I had another girlfriend."

I angrily unbuckled my seatbelt, balled up my fist, grazed my Mama's nose, and punched him in the face. How could he tell such a blasted lie and to my Mama's face! How disrespected I felt.

What happened next shocked me. Instead of my Mama defending me, she started hitting me. I was hurt, embarrassed, and felt humiliated for defending my tarnished reputation.

I would see him on the island from time to time but had little to no interactions with him. Throughout the years when I did see him in passing, he would utter phrases such as "I'm the first to pop your cherry" or "I was your first, remember that." To me, this seemed like the most pathetic thing he could possibly say. And in his mind, that was a grand accomplishment. How sad for him.

Years after I had my son, he later had children with young girls in their teens.

When my son turned a teenager, his father was arrested and not charged for drugging another young high school girl and getting her pregnant. I'm not sure what ever happened with that case; I just know he was set free. This was not a depiction about who I was, but a picture of the man he is. I learned from this experience that he, in fact, had an interest in younger girls, and this glorified the existence of his manhood. It happened to me, but it could have been any vulnerable girl on that island.

It was my decision to choose to not be the victim but a survivor. I chose to not have my son around that unsafe environment and as his mother, to do the best I could for him. Life has a way no matter what you do, and regardless of how much you want better for your children, who they become as an adult may or may not exhibit their genetic makeup.

In my case, this blessing that saved my life is living with a mental health disorder. He has no respect for women and is a physical and verbal abuser. I know this, and I can't protect other women from him.

I used to blame myself. I wondered cruel thoughts about what if my aunts were able to get me that abortion. What did I do wrong? He is my estranged son.

Mental illness is real. I'm compassionate toward his illness. It's not his fault, and I'm forced to love him from a distance. I've done all I can. So, I pray for him, and I pray for myself. To not be a part of his life is painful, and I've learned to cope with these emotions. It's okay for me as a mom to hurt deeply; he is my child. It's also okay for my family and my grandchildren to live mentally well.

Chapter Six: Surviving Domestic Abuse

"The very thing you try to run away from in your past, God has a way of putting that very thing in your path because it was your destiny to overcome it, and not run from it." These words were uttered by my grandmother as she dropped me off at the airport in August 1994. I was twenty-three years old, running for protection from my then-boyfriend. I was badly bruised with scars on the outside, hurt, and I felt like someone took every bone out of my body and shattered them, sucked my blood and only left this terrified, tiny one-hundred-pound shell. I heard her words, but I was not listening because I was so stuck on *Why do bad things always happen to me?* and *Why me, Lord?* Instead, I should have been asking myself, *Lord, what is the lesson you are teaching me?* or *Lord, give me the strength to heal and do right by my children.*

After the birth of my eldest son, I had to undergo a series of surgeries. Just two days before my seventh birthday, I was hit by a car while crossing the street. The car flung me fifty feet and then stopped on my tiny body, where I laid firmly nested under the car's right tire. I could have lost my life, but it was not my time as God had other plans unbeknownst to me. Prior to my son's birth, doctors told me I could not have children because my fallopian tubes were twisted and matted completely shut. But, *God!*

At the age of twenty-three, I moved in with my boyfriend of three years as we wanted to start a family. I listened this time to my grandmother's warning, *"do not to bring another baby into this world living under my roof."* He didn't wait a full day before doing a behavior shift. He started laying down the laws, rules, and regulations as well as the consequences of not following these rules. In my still naïve mind, I thought he was just letting me know that he was the man of the house. It wasn't even a month before the pushing started, followed by the apologies and the words of, "I wish you wouldn't make me so mad."

Sharing a sexual connection was beautiful, blissful, enjoyable, and in most cases, the pleasure and ecstasy of his touch knocked the wind out of me. I wonder how many women remember the day their bundle of joy was conceived. For the second time, my memories of being impregnated led to tears and not of joy.

The day started out great. Watching television and playing around, we shared happy times making love. We ate lunch, and all was well in the world. I remember in the evening, I wanted to make love with him again. He stated that he was going to the car races. This was a hobby of his. I wasn't allowed to go, but before I met him, I used to go all the time. I kissed him goodbye and told him to have fun for both of us.

Midnight came, and as I heard his truck coming up the driveway. I was too excited to see him, and my body was ever so excited as well. As he entered the apartment, his demeanor toward me was that I was bothering him and to leave him alone. I thought maybe he lost money betting on the races. Disappointed, I left him alone and we both fell asleep. His back was to mine, and I faced the wall. Rejection from him was not uncommon. When he felt I was offensive, this was my punishment. I was used to this new behavior since we started living together. I knew that eventually, he would desire me, and when that day came, I'd be ready.

I was awakened in the very early morning hours with him caressing me, craving me, wanting me as I enjoyed every moment of it. The sun was now rising. As the rays shined through the windows on his ever so beautiful honey-glazed, caramel muscular flawless skin, my hands were all over his body.

Then, in slow motion, that one beam of the sun's rays hit his chest and neck. At that moment, my body and my mind shut off like someone turned off the breaker. I laid there frozen as he sat on top of me looking at me blank-faced and clueless as to why I stopped.

You see, as dark and caramelized as his skin was, it couldn't hide a softball sized hickey that was on the left side of his neck. A hickey that clearly, I did not put there. I calmly said, "Go look at your neck in the mirror." He jumped off of me. We were both in the bathroom mirror gazing at the most gigantic hickey. It was big; it should have been measured and listed in the Guinness World Records book.

I stood waiting to hear how he was going to magically lie out of this. All the while inside I was emotionally devastated. After all, it was evident he had sex with another woman. He didn't even shower and then made love to me without one ounce of guilt! Did he not think about my own health or respect me at all? I felt so worthless and broken-hearted. All I could do at that moment was fall to the ground, screaming and crying *Why*?

He remained quiet with guilt. There was no I'm sorry. He was blank. He went back into the bedroom. Hurting, I just cried and cried for hours in the living room.

My emotions were all over the place. He disrespected me and my body. He dishonored our relationship. He dragged my self-worth out the door and kicked it so far that it was beyond the reach of the naked eye. I felt deeply, *Why me?* Between the physical abuse, and now this, how was I going to bounce back from this intense pain?

He finally sat next to me hours later. He stroked my back and said, "I'm sorry I hurt you, but nothing happened. It was just oral sex." I was stargazing at him, having thoughts of how many years of jail I would get for murder. As I had a child to take care of, I really had to talk myself out of my visuals of slowly hurting him to the point of no return.

Now, this fool thinks I'm stupid as well. As dark chocolate as he was, just imagine how long that "oral sex" must have been for her to suck on his neck! She was a human vacuum cleaner!

I got dressed and went down the hill to my Mama. After praying with me, my grandmother told me what most Caribbean women have grown accustomed to. It's only cheating, and that's what men do. Like this was normal, and

I should hurt, heal and go back to him. He was good for you in other ways. You see, out of "shame and feeling worthless" about myself, I never had the strength to tell her he physically abused me. Hurting, I went back even more broken inside.

The hardest thing we must do is to accept our own guilt. When we are faced with a situation, it's not the situation that is relevant, it's our reaction. We are accountable for how we perceive what is in front of us. It's easier to throw the blame on the other person as accepting our own faults can lead to deformation of our own self deeds.

I made that choice to continue to feel worthless, be disrespected and disheartening. At that moment, I had two options. Choose between what I perceived as love for him or to elevate the love for myself and leave an unhealthy situation, knowing that if I stayed it would only get worse. That perceived love was a blindfold for the truth that I didn't want to face. Many times, in my life, being hopeful for others outweighed my love for myself.

Wouldn't you know with just my luck, I was pregnant! That would make the second traumatic conception. I felt stuck, hurt and confused, but I stayed because I thought this was love. If he didn't love me, he would just leave me, but he hasn't. If I stop making him mad, all will be well in the world. I kept this truth of domestic abuse a secret. On the outside, no one knew I was being dragged, punched, and choked because I hid all the bruises. Until the day came the day that made me realize I'd had enough.

My two kids were playing in the bedroom. We returned from Kmart purchasing his son, my second blessing, a pair of sneakers to wear at daycare instead of him wearing his Nike's. You see, he only wanted his son to wear the best, but to me, it didn't make sense for him to wear them to daycare. While in the store, the cashier forgot to take off the second sensor, so the alarm went off at the door. I showed my receipt. They apologized and removed the sensor.

When you live on a small island, folks tend to not mind their own business and are quick to talk about you without knowing all the facts. Someone called him at his job and told him I stole a pair of sneakers. I remember thinking, *Are you serious? Did they forget exactly who my family members are? We can more than afford to buy sneakers! Wait, what!*

Even after showing him the receipt, he still beat me senseless. This time, he went in the kitchen for the knife, grabbed me by my collar, beat me, dragged me around the house and lifted me off the ground. He slammed me against the wall and put the knife to my throat until he drew blood. My arms were dripping bloody and bruised with lacerations. While dangling in midair, I looked down at my two small blessings standing behind him, staring at me, scared. My first blessing actually peed on himself. It was in that moment I said to myself, *God, if you bring me through this, I promise you I am leaving, immediately.*

At that exact moment, he let go and left the house. Just as he left, I grabbed everything I could fit into a suitcase and my two blessings and went to a guy friend's house. My guy friend started the process of sending my car to Florida. He even arranged for friends in Florida to have me stay with them. I went back to my grandmother's house. We were already scheduled to go to Florida on a family vacation three weeks later. The plan, unbeknownst to him, was that we would go on vacation with him, and on the day of departure, inform him that we were *not* returning to St. Thomas with him!

This precise plan included the help of my friends in Florida along with a crew of guys. They let him know that they knew exactly what he did to me, and I was not coming back with him…If he had a problem with that, then they would gladly and forcefully let him understand what was going to happen. While terribly angered, they took him to the airport and watched him aboard the flight. I was *free* and *safe*.

Moving to Florida meant I had to sever ties with friends I had on the island for fear of him trying to find me and harm me. Wherever I went by myself, I found myself checking my surroundings to see if he was following me. If a man simply opened the door to the grocery store or restaurant, I would jump out of my skin. His abuse affected me. Sometimes, I would call him and hang up. Not that I wanted him back, but more like checking to see if he was still alive. I silently hoped that he wasn't as this is what abuse does to your thoughts.

I was torn between letting him be a part of his son's life or whether it would benefit or hurt my son if he knew the truth about his father.

I invited him a couple of years later to visit us. Despite who he was, I wanted him to know his son. I obtained my black belt in karate and learned how to defend myself, which also included a license to carry a firearm. Things were well until it wasn't, and again, I had to force him to leave by calling the police. People are who they are.

I self-coped by emotionally moving on with my life and pushed on with my son, who was with me, and my other son who would later come live with us once we were settled into our new life.

I didn't receive therapy for the abuse, but I should have. I never thought that physical abuse was a form of a mental health disorder. Feeling empowered, as I now can defend myself, I willed myself to believe that everything will be okay. Despite the years of nightmares of him beating me and the distrust I had for men, I tried to push past unsuccessfully that negative view of all men. In my world, having a relationship meant being physically hurt. I had the false notion that if I just focused on my child and ignored all hurt, then all would be well.

Chapter Seven: Married Life

In life, we never know where the experiences we encounter will lead. They may lead to a very rewarding, joyful, and happy ending. I don't think it's ever a person's intention to enter relationships with the intention of it coming to an end. Until this point in my life, different things kept blocking my path toward finding myself. This segment of my journey will give you a glimpse into my world as a married woman and how my now- ex-husband became my now-best friend, and the amazing father God intended for him to be to our kids.

In 1996, I was excited that I closed on my first home in Pembroke Pines, our very own two-bedroom townhouse. Life finally started feeling normal. Now a mother of two, my eldest son at this time lived in the Virgin Islands with my Mama. My youngest son AJ, just three years old, lived with me. I had no other choice but to separate the boys. In life, as mothers, we have to make some really tough decisions and just pray in the long run everything works out in the best interest for our children.

I had just landed a job working as an administrative assistant for an investigation company that conducted background checks. I was also going into my junior year for yet another degree, my bachelor's in computer science.

My soon to be husband, Mark Young worked in the Information Technology Department. This meant he already knew everything about me as he was in charge of setting up all my credentials and my computer in the company. He knew that my birthday is on December sixth. He may have already had some sort of crush on me. One day as I was working on the company's database file, he stopped by and smiled. Then he said, "Hey, I'm a Sagittarius, too, and my birthday is December seventh!" I was like, ah, okay, and smiled back.

My supervisor, Jennifer, let's just call her Miss Cupid, started telling me how wonderful a guy he is. She encouraged him to ask me out. Clueless me, I wasn't sure what was going on. So, I thought, *What in the what*? I'm not sure if you understand how much I dislike being put on the spot. It feels like my space has been invaded.

One day, he purchased lunch and invited me to eat with him. We sat outside in the employee's tropical oasis eating area. It felt like a picnic on the beach, minus the water. As we sat on the concrete bench, there was an umbrella over us; it was very cozy and comfortable. At that moment, I viewed it as he was being friendly and a gentleman. It was a very nice gesture, and I was thankful.

He asked a lot of questions as he wanted to get to know me, I supposed. I was in a place in my life where shame was imbedded very deeply inside. My answers were very short and vague. Knowing the man I know today, this gesture took every ounce of bravery to do.

You see, Mark is very shy and not one to get his temper tested. He's a brilliant introvert and the type of man who stays to himself. He's focused on his career, not about drama, as he has to be calm and low key for the type of work he does. I didn't know this at the time.

I only allowed him into my school life. We had a connection as I was in the process of studying the same career path he was already on, computer networking and programming. The internet had just launched, and it piqued both of our talents and interests.

Within just a few short months, I was promoted, working in his department alongside his older brother John. Here I was, an African American woman, climbing into the ceiling, running cables and building computers from parts, installing Cisco routers, and installing Microsoft Software even though I had not finished college.

In this era, I was the only woman in my classes as I studied information technology at Florida Atlantic University while working for a predominantly Caucasian firm. I loved this new endeavor, but I was still clueless that he was seriously into me even though he had taken me out to dinner several times and helped me to study. I viewed him as a good friend, the only guy friend I had.

With his assistance, patience, and confidence in me, I passed my A-plus certification exam and became Microsoft Certified in Networking, Office and NT. In the computer field at that time, that was major. It was the end of DOS 3.0 and the beginning of Windows. We were both at the top of our careers in less than a year.

To celebrate our victories, he took me out for wings and drinks with my toddler. I was beginning to feel whole and accomplished. For most of my teen and young adult life, I've been the responsible mother that hardly drank alcohol. I might have enjoyed myself just a little bit too much. He ended up driving us home. One thing leads to another, and then the condom broke with me screaming "Oh my, I'm pregnant!" Next was a complete blur.

In October, he took me to the airport where he loves watching planes take off and land. There, he took a knee and asked me to marry him. Like I said before, I really dislike being put on the spot. I really admired him. I could speak to him about anything. His mind intrigued me. He was what every other man was not. He was the definition of what a man should be. He would do anything for me. He loved me. I knew he would never hit me. Since I was a victim of domestic abuse in my previous relationship, this thought had to be added into my mental checklist.

I knew he would be a great provider. In my mind, before I answered, I went down a checklist to convince myself to say yes. Not that I loved him but screamed out "Yes!" Did you notice that me saying I loved him was not on that list? How could it? My view of love had been totally distorted by my past.

The following month, guess who was pregnant with my third child? Why me, of course, because that was my life's journey!

He was ecstatic to be a father. He was already a great role model for my second son, AJ. He was even happier to be a husband and have our together family. I, on the other hand, was sick every day, miserable and disappointed in the entire situation. I felt like for the third time in a row I'd been just tossed into motherhood. I went back to hating myself because that made me feel normal. Hating myself was so common to me that it was easier to just stay there. I wondered why must my children be conceived in a manner that was not normal. Not realizing or owning that the journey that is my life was never ordained to be of the norm, but for a greater more powerful reason unbeknownst to me. So, I wrapped up in my own selfishness to see anything good.

He was a good man and a great provider an overall gentleman. I was my own problem in the equation, but in my view, he was the problem.

Two months pregnant and living together in December, I was so sick that I could barely make it off the bed. He cooked, took care of AJ, cleaned, and took care of me. There was no hiding my pregnancy from my employer. Unfortunately, the job had a no fraternization policy, which meant I had to quit, and I lost my insurance.

Things were just getting worse as far as I looked at it. I had to leave a job that I loved and was good at to stay home being sick, pregnant, and with a toddler. Mark accepted his responsibilities out of love. Love came easily for him, but not for me.

I was becoming sicker and sicker daily to where I was having contractions every day. This child did not want to stay in my body! The doctor placed me as high-risk, and to avoid giving birth meant removing and stapling my vagina closed every two weeks. Oh, the agony, soreness, and pain. I was determined and focused on carrying this baby to term as I could not carry another child because my body was just not cooperating. Things were the ultimate hell on earth from my viewpoint.

Not wanting the risk of me not having health insurance, we went to the courthouse and got married, as I continued to plan our big wedding ceremony in April. Planning the wedding honestly helped me to cope.

I hated being pregnant, I hated being sick all day long, I hated not being able to move off the bed, and I hated this new life. I hated my doctor! I hated everything except my children and my baby who was in my belly.

Now that I look back, this man calmly put up with my misery every day. After a hectic day, he'd come home to my complaints and my woe-is-me attitude. Yet, he never appeared bothered. He took everything in stride.

I doubt during that time that I ever asked him how his day was. Yet still, he loved me.

Our wedding day came. It was the only time my granny flew on a plane to visit me in my lifetime. She was not going to miss this moment despite her fear of flying. I was so happy, not because I was getting married but because my grandma came to see me and told me that everything was going to be okay. I willed myself to believe this was just wedding jitters.

As I write this, I'm crying because he didn't deserve this. He deserved love in return. He was so happy to marry the woman he loved in the presence of his family and friends. Yet, I'm was my dress thinking just get this day over with, so I can lie down because I was pregnant, constantly nauseous and in pain.

My family stayed to watch the boys for two days. I couldn't fly in my condition for both my health and our baby. For our honeymoon, we decided to rent a beautiful cottage in the woods of Georgia. He had to drive some twenty-four hours with me stopping constantly, and he had to deal with my nasty, miserable attitude.

Just give him the "Man of the Decade" award! Now that I'm reflecting back to that time, Phew!

By my eighth month, he had no option but to take care of both children as my eldest son now lived with us. He went to work every day non-stop and then came home to do everything for me, including giving me a bath. I was completely disabled. In addition, this bundle of painful joy stayed awake when I needed to sleep.

Throughout my pregnancy, the doctor conducted eight sonograms that all showed I was having a boy. Yet, I was convinced they were all wrong and that this baby was a girl.

Finally, the day came to bring my miracle baby into the world. Mark's entire family came to the hospital. This was a complete contrast to my previous children's births, which I did alone.

When the doctors said, "It's a boy," I said to put him back in as she isn't finished.

Mark cut the cord, and Marik Young entered into the world, drugged, distressed and severely jaundiced. Machines beeped loudly. I was in and out of consciousness due to the medication, and my eyelids wanted to shut down. I was in no condition to even hold my child. Mark kissed me on my forehead and told me to get some rest and that he would make sure Riki (this is the nickname we gave to our son) was okay. I was confused and felt like I was floating in the clouds. I asked, "Does he have any birthmarks?"

That's the only way I could think of to ensure that he was my baby when it was time for me to hold him. Mark said, "Yes, he has the island of St. Thomas on his left arm by his elbow." I laughed, and that's the last thing I remembered.

When I awoke, I was in the recovery room. My husband was not there. Instead, there was my doctor and a social worker. Puzzled, I instantly thought the worst and that something happened to my baby! The doctor proceeded to ask me if I was sure that my husband was my son's father. Upset and unnerved, I quickly cursed at him. They were both trying to calm me down. I'm told the reason I was so sick my entire pregnancy was caused by my placenta had a rip. My baby not only had a rare RH Factor, but also the sickle cell trait. His blood type was also B Negative. My baby's blood was slowly leaking into my O positive blood, and for nine months, my body rejected his blood.

My medical records stated that both Mark and I have O positive, so there was no possible way he could be his father. I've never been so happy to see Mark's mother, Eva, as she sharply walked in and said that's her son's blood type. Let's just say she saved the doctor from meeting the Caribbean side of me. Pain or not, I was ready to grab someone and knock some sense into them. They needed to bring me, my baby!

They told me his liver failed while I was sleeping due to high levels of jaundice. He was stable and under the Bili lights.

Bili lights are a type of light therapy (phototherapy) that are used to treat newborn jaundice. Jaundice is a yellow coloring of the skin and eyes. It is caused by too much of a yellow substance called bilirubin. Bilirubin is created when the body replaces old red blood cells with new ones.

The mood I was in, I didn't care! I kept repeating and insisting they needed to bring me, my child!!!

The nurse brought the entire Bili lights infant bed with my baby into my room just to keep me at bay.

The nurse placed Riki on my chest. I could not see his eyes as I went searching for his birthmark. There it was just as Mark described it. While exhaling, a sudden burst of emotions entered my soul, and I began crying. I was so happy to hold this little bugger that had me a total, complete mess for nine months. I was so in love with him, his smell, and his skin, so soft against my cheek. Longing to see his eyes, I removed the Bili glasses. Wouldn't you know this newborn looked right at me as if to say "Hey, Mom; there you are," and smiled.

I was in total amazement as my other children did not open their eyes on day one like this.

After his birth and for my health, I had to make the decision to tie, cut, as well as burn my fallopian tubes. It's not typical that doctors do all three, but we needed to ensure that never again in my lifetime should another egg pass though my tubes or I could lose my life.

I didn't want to believe that God would not bless me with a girl to continue my legacy. That was a painful decision I had to make. My children needed me alive and well, so I had to do what I was instructed to do for them.

We came home to our bedroom, now converted to cater to Riki's jaundice needs. For almost two months, he lived under the Bili lights. In addition, every morning Mark had to take our baby for a forty-five-minute drive round trip to get Riki's blood tested. During the work week, he would turn right around and drive about an hour to work.

Here I was, a mother of three children, a newborn, a five-year-old, and an eleven-year-old who was not accepting of having two brothers, and who was acting out. I was just grateful that for the first time in months, I felt better.

Mark took a couple of weeks off from work, which really just meant he worked from home. I was grateful as it was August, which meant no school.

I slowly adjusted to motherhood. After summer ended, I was ready to go back to work. Due to my vast knowledge of computers, I found another job quickly as the Management Information Technology Administrator for the Department of Health. I was back in my happy place with work and my children, but still not content with my life—especially being a wife.

On one of our anniversaries, not sure if it was year one or two, I told him, "I don't think I can love you." I could see the hurt in his eyes, but I was too stuck in my own selfishness to care. Not giving up on my marriage and not wanting to hurt him, I stayed.

In 2000, we purchased a bigger single-story house together just two miles west of my townhouse.

Unbeknownst to me, I was falling back into self-hatred and doubt. As for everyone around, they thought we had a life they would love to have. Every holiday weekend, we traveled out of town. We appeared to be happy, but inside I was miserable. Mark came home, cooked, and then sat on the computer and worked until he went to bed. He connected computers, so the boys and he could play computer games together.

My life consisted of getting the boys ready for school, going to work all day, picking them up from after school activities, completing homework, bathing, and putting them to bed.

While they all played video games, I felt bored and left out. Not one of my boys liked shopping. The word "shop" disgusted all of them. I was the only Y chromosome in the house. On weekends, they would play all day long.

My wanting to have a girl became a desperate desire and need. My girlfriends all had girls. Being around them made me feel like God was punishing me, so I stayed away.

If I saw a baby or toddler girl anywhere, I felt worse about myself. I felt less than a woman despite the fact that I had everything and more right in front of me.

Early in 2001, the entire family went inside Kmart for groceries. They had rearranged the store, which meant we had no other choice but to walk through the infant girl's clothing section. I fell to the ground, and out of the blue, started hysterically crying.

Mark was concerned that something physically happened to me. I think he realized what had happened when he looked around at the clothes and then told the boys we need to get your mom home, now!

As soon as the minivan pulled up, I ran into our master bathroom, locked the door and called my grandmother. I poured my heart out to her. I told her my womanhood was gone. I can't have another child. The boys and my husband made me feel so left out and alone. At that moment, I expressed how incomplete I felt. She and I prayed together. I can only imagine how helpless she must have felt. When I opened the bathroom door, there my husband stood in tears.

I must have really stepped out of myself. He hated seeing me so unhappy. What he said next to this day still gives me goosebumps.

He said, "Let's adopt; let me give you this gift you need."

I hugged him so tight and then ran to the computer to start searching on information on adopting in Florida.

The process of adoption in Florida turned out to be a complete nightmare. It was as if they didn't want us to adopt. They wanted their vision of what a perfect family should look like. Oh, you can't imagine the roadblocks they put in our path.

Frustrated, we decided to look into international adoption. We searched online for countries that allowed US citizens to adopt. We decided on China. Their government has two children in the house rule added to the fact that if their first child happened to be a girl, the family would give their daughter up for adoption. This was mind-blowing to me.

While looking for a US agency to facilitate our adoption, we stumbled on this agency that had a flashing sign with the words "Cambodia now open." We both looked at each other as to say, "Why is Cambodia open?"

As we researched Cambodia on March 19th, 2001, our hearts sank. We read information about the Khmer Rouge that lead that country into genocide. It was evident that this was indeed the country we should adopt from. We had to not only adopt for our own needs, but we needed to make a difference in one child's life.

Faith would have it, and God had planned it to be this way as our daughter was born on that exact date halfway around the world in Cambodia, Asia.

When we received a picture of our daughter in May with her birthday stamped, we felt this was God's doing! My happiness within myself returned. We were going to complete our family with this beautiful baby. The boys were so excited. Every step we took, we included them. This was not their adopted sister. She was going to be their baby sister forever.

The moment we saw and held our baby girl was just the same as the day we held and welcomed our son into the world.

I quit my nine-to-five job permanently to raise our four children. This meant Mark had to take on more work. We saw him less and less—maybe one day a week when he played video games with the boys while I went shopping with my daughter.

At this point, I began once again to hate myself and self-doubt returned. I felt like I was raising the children by myself, and it was putting a toll on me physically and emotionally. I expressed to my husband how I was feeling.

and he responded that he felt as if nothing he did ever seemed enough for me to be happy.

Defensively, I felt like my feelings did not matter to him. All he wanted to do was work. I felt like he was working all the time to get away from me. I started to drift apart emotionally from him as I didn't think there was a way for him to see that work came first and his family came second. Nothing I said or did could make him see what I was telling him.

My marriage for sure was failing. We were strangers in our home. I didn't want to share the same air that he breathed.

We unintentionally placed our daughter in a beauty pageant just for fun, and it turned out she came alive on the stage. Not wanting to be home with him on the weekends when he did take a day off, I entered our daughter in every beauty pageant available. This was my new happy place.

He didn't seem to mind that I found something that made me feel happy. He was happy for me. Sometimes he and the boys would come and show support for our daughter. They would cheer, jump, and scream in the audience for her. They were so proud of her.

After a while, I started to compete with my daughter. I felt my self-hate and doubt vanishing away completely. It felt great being on stage again.

Just as I did in my younger years to hide how ugly I felt on the outside while dying inside, feeling worthless from verbal, physical and emotional abuse, pageantry and modeling was my temporary Band-Aid to put me in my happy place. Appearing to be happy was normal in my world.

I found myself addicted to the facade of smiles and poise. I sat on the computer for hours trying to find the next pageant to enter.

Mark paid for all of our pageant expenses, flight, hotel, clothing, and entry fees. Every weekend, I was spending thousands of dollars. It was not until I started competing did he start to complain about money. I felt he was jealous that I'd found something I loved. So deep in my own selfishness, I couldn't see that pageantry had taken over my world and was draining our bank accounts. Yes, I was still mom during the week, but my mind was focused more on the upcoming pageants.

My children had two parents with a love for things occupying our time outside of the house. Mark had his job, and I had my pageantry. Still, he appeared happy for me until I won Mrs. World Beauty, and that's when reality hit. This pageant took place in Texas, which meant he would have all four of the children. It was very rare that I left him alone with all four of the children simply because he was always at work.

He was not at all happy when he dropped me off at the airport. I think secretly he hoped I would lose. When I did call him to tell him that I won, he did not answer the phone.

He found out after I landed and was sitting on the curb at the airport with my crown on. He did not say anything to me as he placed my bags in the trunk. No congratulations. He was cold as if he was a taxi driver picking up another passenger.

At that moment, I checked out of my marriage completely. The more distant I became, the more hours he worked. Neither of us saw how much this was hurting our children.

I filed for divorce, and what I did next was purely out of spite and anger and the ultimate level of selfishness. I had my attorney serve him divorce papers in a box of chocolates at the place I felt was his first love—his job. In my mind, this was a really great idea until it turned out to be the biggest mistake I'd ever made.

Deeply hurt people can deeply hurt other people. Mark cleaned out all of our bank accounts and stopped paying the mortgage, utilities, and food. I didn't plan for that to happen. He then disappeared somewhere in Florida. The only time we saw him was in court during our divorce for four long years, fighting me on everything.

Once divorced, he packed up and moved out of state, leaving the three children in Florida by ourselves with no child support and no job. My eldest son has been on his own since he turned seventeen. I managed to sell the house before it was foreclosed. There, we were broke and homeless. Our only option was to move back to the Virgin Islands.

Forgiveness

I stayed in the Virgin Islands for only three months but was more miserable than ever and felt like a total, complete failure. My grandmother hated seeing me this way and was concerned about my mental state. She insisted I move back to Florida and leave the boys with my uncle since they offered and take my daughter with me to start over with her help and blessings.

Besides those few days of competing in Texas, I've never left my boys' side and the thought sickened me. My world was a wreck, but my children have always been my lifeline. How could I survive without them? Truth is that I was not surviving with them. The stress of the divorce was taking a toll on my body.

I developed two huge goiters in my throat. Not sleeping at night, I developed severe insomnia. Not sure how as I stopped eating, but I gained almost fifty pounds.

At the airport, I waved, with my eyes full of tears, at my boys, promising them I'd be back in a year.

Taking off on a plane and leaving my children behind felt like someone pulled all of my limbs apart slowly in agonizing pain, and I died inside.

I used all that pain to rebuild myself. The judge ordered therapy for myself and my daughter. Hesitant and left with no other option, I sat in front of a therapist for the first time in my life. Filled with anger, hurt, a failure as a mother, wife and as a woman, I had reached rock bottom.

I was either going to accept the help and get my life together or... I'm not even sure what the other option was for me. I couldn't envision it as there was no other option! To me, the only other option was death, and that was not an option. I needed to get my boys back in the states with me.

I kept my promise, and a year later, and many therapy sessions I learned so much about myself. All the times I thought that my forgetfulness was age related it was not. Turned out that I was living with Adult Attention Deficit Disorder. It felt like I had to relearn how to live again in a brand-new way. I had a clearer version of my life, knowing the reason as to why my conversations and thoughts can go from one extreme to another. It answered the questions as to why I can't stay on task. Ultimately making me a better mother.

I flew back to St. Thomas and moved my boys back to Florida with me. Life was a little better than being homeless and broke. We lived in the projects on government assistance, and I was working a job that paid only nine dollars an hour. It was a far cry from making sixty thousand a year. In any event, I was determined that as long as we had each other, we were going to be just fine.

Therapy painfully showed me how much of a selfish, self-centered, mean woman I'd become. That self-revaluation that makes you accountable for your life feels awful, and yet it's the very thing I needed to bounce back. I resisted discussing my mother's illness, which meant I truly did not want to be fully healed. We discussed everything else, but my mother and father were off limits.

I didn't want to admit that my problem was me not fully accepting all of my own painful truths and that I chose to continue to let others define who I was. I was upset every time my therapist mentioned anything about my mother. There were times I stormed off and walked out the door, but still returning for the next visit.

Had I known then what I know now, I should have spoken to her about my life with my mother. My moment of being emotionally free happened when I accepted help to overcome the internal pain, I lived with for over forty years of my life. If I never received and accepted the hold her illness had on me, I wouldn't be writing this second book or experience the joy that I have for myself in this present moment.

It's not emotionally healthy to let the fear of your past circumstances dictate the outcome of your future self. For me, I had to go as far back as possible to when I was three years old and forgive myself. This may sound easy, but it's one of the hardest things I've ever had to face. It was not something that I did, nor did something happen to me. I had to learn how to forgive myself for how I felt at such a young age. That was my first memory of me hating my mother for not being like the other mothers. This subconscious memory lingered with me most of my life.

Once I discovered the main reasons that caused me to have so much self-hate, it opened the door for healing. It became clear that I needed to forgive myself for every event in my life. Again, not easy, but extremely necessary. This meant forgiving my ex-husband. At the time I was in therapy; he was losing his mother to cancer.

I realized in therapy that he, just like I, had to learn to go without our children to see exactly where we needed to be for them.

Absence makes the heart grow fonder. His children missed him just as much as he missed them. He and I spoke our truths, pains, and apologies. We started out doing it just for the sake of our children. Our entire life, he kept me whole. We started out as really great friends, and then life threw us on a roller coaster ride. On that ride, we were still each other's friend, but during the entire ride, I made it unbearable toward the end.

We need to be in each other's lives for us. The children are the blessings we share together. He painfully had to learn how to balance work and family. The distance between our children brought him to become more involved and closer to them. He has never missed a precious moment in their lives even though he lives three states and six hours away.

What we have always shared is not romantic or sexual; it's fulfilling love. How many of us have someone you can discuss every single aspect in your life with...without judgment?

I used to wonder what if I had been healed before I was married, could or would I ever love him? That thought has not crossed my mind since he came back into our lives. We are right where God intended us to be.

My daughter and I will always be his girls. He will forever be my guy. Love doesn't have to look the same for everyone. It just has to feel right to you.

Chapter Eight: I fell in love with a Married Man

Whenever I read a post on Facebook or hear someone condemning a woman for being with a married man, I swallow a pill of guilt, then release it. I used to be very ashamed. What if you simply didn't know he was married? This is my journey untold, totally unscripted and totally unplanned. Things just happen in my world.

Three years after settling in with three of my kids in Orlando, I decided to sign up on Match, the dating app. The place that supposedly only singles go. I went on a few dates but had no connection. I was about to disable my account as I felt that I clearly had no clue what men in Orlando wanted, and from my experience, most men in that area are looking for women to run after them or sit and wait for them to have time for you. I'm just not that type of woman. I run after or wait on no man.

In my inbox, there was his message. He was light skinned with hazel eyes.

After two weeks of speaking with him over the phone. We decided to meet at Froggers for dinner. The smile on his face as he walked in melted my heart. I had never seen any one man thus far before so delighted to meet me.

We ate, talked, and laughed for so long that we closed down the restaurant. That's how good the connection was. He opened doors, was a gentleman, and walked me to my car. Chivalry did not die with him.

He spoke with so much conviction in his voice, looking dead in my eyes with his beautiful hazel-brown eyes and said he was single and an executive for a very well-known company. He said that his kids' mother lived in Tampa with his teen twin boys. He traveled on most weekends to see his kids, usually on a Friday and returned to the Orlando area the next day. I was grateful that he shared this information upfront with me. After all, I'm happy to see a man find a balance and be a part of his kids' lives despite the distance.

He also mentioned that he travels for his job to different cities, one in particular located in Virginia.

On our next date, he showed up in a red BMW, a different car than what he told me he owned. He owned a blue Lexus. Curiously, I asked if he owned two cars and he said he did. Another great evening, which lead to our first kiss in the parking lot. His kiss was simply magical. We didn't want to leave each other that night.

After a few months, things began to get serious between us. One Friday, before he left for Tampa to see his kids, he stopped by to tell me that he made an appointment for me, fully paid, to get a massage and my nails filled on Saturday. In my forty something years of my life, no other man had ever done that. You're probably wondering about what kind of men I've dated in my life. I'm forty-eight as I'm writing this, and he is, to this day, still the only man to do this for me. Most men I've encountered do not understand this is what a busy, working woman needs. Just go the extra step and do the things we tend to neglect, which is self-maintenance. At least this working woman needs this!

My attraction toward him grew from this small gesture. As he pulled out of the driveway, waving goodbye to each other, he gazed at me with his charismatic smile and I knew I was falling deeper for him.

He always called when he arrived. I woke up to his morning messages every day. He would also text or call me when he was on the way back. As soon as he arrived back into Orlando, the preparation and planning started for us to spend time together.

After six months, I allowed him to meet my three children and they immediately liked him. He was funny and had an infectious, charismatic, witty personality. I loved that my kids liked him as this was important to me. We are a unit; you're not just dating me. You're dating all of us.

We would go to the beach often as a family. He took us out to nice restaurants to eat, bought us groceries and items for my kids. You name it, and as a man, he really did more than most men have.

He pampered and spoiled me. I'm talking about earrings costing thousands and name brand clothing—over the top elaborate gifts. He had to remind me daily to embrace this treatment as this is how a woman should be treated.

He would draw my hot baths and lavish me in ways as you see on television, like lingerie in pretty-wrapped boxes, chocolates on the bed, and huge beautiful bouquets with my favorite flowers just because. Hhhmmm, now that I'm writing this, I'm thinking how he raised the bar very high and maybe that's why I'm still single. No other man has leveled up to the type of treatment he blessed us with. I have hope!

With the presentation of every gift, flowers, etc., I felt unworthy as if it was all too much, instead of embracing them. At this point in my life, I was trying to find my own way. I needed to find my purpose and become my own version of a successful woman.

We met right after my father passed away in the year 2010. The timing was perfect as I felt my parents' left me here in this world alone. I was still grieving over both of their back-to-back years of loss. Here was my center beam to hold this damaged, hurtful soul of my existence together.

I did notice different patterns and red flags, but I kept them to myself. As a child, I was taught that if a man is treating you right, let the goodness outweigh everything else. Bad advice that I never passed on to my children, thankfully. The biggest red flag I often wondered after being at his condo many times was where was the red BMW?

Some other flags were raised. Where and who were his male friends? Where was his family? Did they not check up on him? In my presence, he barely ever touched his phone. He was solely focused on my kids and me. Our perfect little family, I thought.

After nine months into our relationship, I finally asked him about the red BMW. He stumbled as he said, it's in storage and there was no need to drive it in the city because he only drove it on long trips or to Tampa. Why would I not believe that? It sounded realistic, right? He was preserving the vehicle from everyday wear and tear, it seemed. I had the kids with me most of the time, so we did not go on trips with just the two of us. So why wouldn't he take me for a drive in it?

In those nine months, he traveled five times for work. However, while on those trips, he barely answered my calls. He would text and let me know he was in a meeting or a conference. Most of the times he returned my calls in the night hours to let me know he loved me and wished me goodnight. He would include me in his business world and enlighten me on how the conferences went and what they were about. Sometimes, he would send me pictures of other people attending the conferences.

Again, this seemed plausible and realistic. He was just busy and being a businesswoman, many times after I've attended a conference, I would unwind in my hotel room with a glass of wine. I didn't feel like speaking to anyone and just drifted away with a clear mind for the next day.

Another pondering red flag was that not once did he speak to his kids' mother in my presence. Again, I didn't see this as a sign. I don't call my ex-husband when I'm around the person I'm seeing, either. They are exes for a reason.

The entire time we were together, I never met his kids. Many times, he had to travel to Tampa for court as his ex-wife often wanted more child support. I even went to the courthouse with him and waited outside of the courtroom. What a wonderful, supportive girlfriend I was. Now, I'm lamenting, those were long trips so why did we not drive the red BMW?

He helped me start my women's clothing line: Let's Journey into Fashion. We both wanted to own a boutique store. He had the funds, and I had the online business knowledge. We were a perfect blend. I've always desired to have a relationship that would allow us to be lovers and business partners. Winning!

While I didn't have a conversation about the things with him that were red flags to me, I did share them with my bestie (guy best friend). Many times, my bestie told me something seemed off, and that he was too perfect. Defensive, I was thinking that he was just hating. Boy, was I wrong!

A year into the relationship, we traveled to St. Thomas, my hometown, for carnival. I knew he was here before with his "ex-wife" as he did mention this early on. While on the island, which he was very familiar, we met some people who were still around since his last visit. Everything about that trip was awesome! In my view, how much more perfect could our lives be? I was in love, happy, peaceful, and full of bliss.

Upon returning, the marriage talks began as well as moving in together.

A few weeks after our island getaway, my paternal grandmother passed away. I was devastated. This would make it a three-peat, back-to-back-to-back years of loss and grief in my family. From the moment I found out, on Facebook of all places, he was there through all my emotions of anger, family drama, and frustrations. We flew back to St. Thomas with my last son. Mr. Wonderful stood by my side at the funeral. He is even pictured in the family photos at the gravesite.

However, on this trip, he was rather unnerved. We stayed at my house on St. John, which meant no cell coverage or WIFI for a few days.

When I confronted him and questioned what was wrong, he said, "It was work or he could not reach his kids." With two of my own children in Florida, I totally understood. I was concerned as well, but not unnerved. I knew they were okay.

When we made it back to St. Thomas, he told me he was upset at his ex-wife. I didn't intrude. I felt it was not my business. All I could do in those moments was to be as empathetic as possible.

Once we got back to Orlando, he said that he had to leave for Tampa because his children needed him. However, this visit was not the norm. There were no calls or texts. My instinct said something was not right. Being the trusting person that I am, I thought something physically happened to him. I was even upset that there was no communication, but my main concern was that I wanted to know that he was not hurt.

A few days later, he came to my house. I was so relieved that he was okay that I forgot I'd been so upset. He apologized and told me that before we moved forward with moving in there was something, he needed to tell me. What he said, I was not ready for. Thinking back, I'm really surprised I didn't hurt him physically.

When the words, "I'm married but we are going through a divorce," touched my eardrums, my brain didn't register it. I said, "Come again?" *Say what? You are who? What in the what?* Have you ever stepped out of your body and saw yourself having an "Oh, hell, nah" followed by a full-blown

Madea moment? You are yelling at the person and pacing back and forth with your arms flying in the air, but instead, your body just stands frozen from shock?

I thought *I am being punked* anytime now, and the cameras would come out and everyone would yell "Surprise!"

His rationale for not telling me. This man stood in front of me and told me that it was my fault since I told him in conversations from day one that I could never be with a married man!"

You read that right. My fault!

At that moment, my brain said, *so you knew this was my position from day one, and yet you felt you would be the decision-maker of my life.* You chose to break my own rules for me and do what you pleased for your own selfishness. You put my reputation in jeopardy. You put my standards for myself on the floor, stamped all over them, and disrespect my morals and me?

My mouth, probably for the first time in my life, said nothing. I just stood there with a blank, scary stare, thinking this has to be someone else's life. God wouldn't do this to me after what I've been through already with men.

He then admitted that the court hearings were not for child support after all but for their divorce case.

My self-thoughts registered, *Wait, we have even more lies*! Well, what kind of fool I had truly been all this time.

The only words I could muster at this point were "Get the hell out of my house!!"

Have you ever been so hurt, and your world was turned upside down that you couldn't even comprehend, and your eyes couldn't shed a single tear? My entire body was shaking. My head was spinning. My kids were speaking, and I heard nothing. To really describe it into words, my body was on the couch, but my soul went for a very long, confusing, figuratively speaking, walk out-of-the-country to dissect and digest all of the lies.

I had questions that needed answers. What in the? How in the? What just happened? The biggest question would make my heart feel like it was going to burst in my chest. How could I have been so blind and stupid to not see or know any of this!

I turned to my bestie, who, for the first time in his life, went silent. We were both in shock. He said, "I know something felt off but didn't think an entire wife." He then told me if I really needed answers, a discussion must occur. If I needed to just walk away without knowing, then he suggested that is what I should do, but also said, "Whichever decision you make, it's up to you." Whichever one I made, he will always be there for me, always!

I honestly don't recall how long it took me to find the courage to contact him as he had been trying to reach out to me, but I had blocked him.

In any event, I remember distinctly when we were sitting on my bed and he showed me the text messages from his kids' mother, aka "The Wife," discussing some intense divorce conversations. I sat there reading every word.

Love said, "Yes, this man has been good to you. Give him some credit. He told you because he wants to move forward with you. Yes, he lied, but he is sitting here apologizing. Find forgiveness."

My inner self-thoughts screamed, *Run! This is some bullshit! These aren't little tales. These are gigantic bold-faced lies! Heffa, kick his ass! Go in the yard, break off a tree limb, and just go all in on his ass!*

Unfortunately, I listened to love. Women and our damn emotions—they get the best of us. I stayed because there was evidence of divorce and the fact that when I did unblock him and read all of the messages, he was sorry and didn't mean to hurt me. He professed that I was the one he loved and wanted to be with, and so he had to tell me the truth, knowing it would hurt me. From my standpoint, it looked as if he really did love me and wanted to finally end that chapter and move forward with our lives, or so I thought. The plot thickened!

As we both tried to move forward, the more of a hypocrite I felt. A guilty conscience, self-doubt, and self-hatred moved in. This is the one thing I would not dare tell my maternal grandmother (my granny). She would throw the Bible at me with the binder edge just to leave a big dent in my dumb skull. I told my grandmother everything, but I would not dare tell her any of this. Judgement from a Christian God-loving woman on this matter, I felt, would be the utmost. The longer I stayed, the sicker I became emotionally.

Despite my feelings, we went house shopping. We found a four-bedroom house to rent. It was very nice and just the right size. My intuition told me not to put my name on that lease, and when the day came to sign, I didn't show. He signed the lease without me, so the house was in his name only.

He was so mad at me, and yet, I couldn't have cared less. As far as my mindset was concerned, he would have to move on; I was not ready nor healed from his lies. I refused to move in even though it was still an option. The saying, "Let your conscience be your guide" spoke to me loudly and daily.

We planned a getaway to New York for a week. He felt we needed a trip, finally. I felt he needed a good ass whooping with a bat from me, but that's against the law. Keep in mind, emotionally, I was still in disarray and flustered. Prior to this trip, I never posted any pictures of us on social media or mentioned our relationship outside of my close friends and family. I decided it was time. I posted a picture from the airport of us in the taxi of him smiling ear-to-ear proud and happy to be there with me. I even tagged him. Well, what unfolded next, not even Lifetime Channel editors could write about.

As I said at the beginning of this chapter, only in my world do things like this happen.

First, let me remind you how tagging on Facebook worked back then. By default, settings were set to friends and friends of those friends. Even though "The Wife" was not on his Facebook page, his sons were.

Who do you think saw the picture? Yup, the wife! She proceeded to send me a message asking me why I was in New York on a business trip with her husband.

He was sitting right next to me, and I said nothing. My thoughts, however, said *business trip*. I could feel his phone vibrating next to me. I said innocently and calmly, "You should get that. It might be important." He replied, "Nothing is more important than us right now." Then he kissed me on my forehead. I think I vomited in my mouth at his comment and gave him a royal Caribbean woman's cut eye as if to say, without words, whatever the hell, you liar.

Have you ever had a let the devil get his moment? That's the state I was in. Just six more days next to this lying good for nothing man. I can pull off this facade.

I did not respond to her that day, but I watched to see how he would respond to all her missed calls and texts. He didn't touch his phone. He placed it on silent. I figured this much as she was cursing me out in all her messages to me. One message said. "Tell my husband to answer his fucking phone."

Let's get something straight in this situation; I'm the unsuspecting victim of this web of deception. I calmly wrote her back that he had been lying to both of us for a very long time and gave her my phone number to call me. I had no idea what I would say if she actually did call. I hadn't thought that far out.

I went downstairs to the lobby to take her call. After her very loud, foul cursing and yelling, I calmly asked her if she cared to listen to me. I told her everything, especially the part about the divorce text. She seemed unknowing of any such text and called me a liar and worse. My guilt cup runneth over this day. I hated myself times infinity. As she asked, "What kind of woman is so low to be with a married man?" I asked myself the same question, but in my hand held a hammer pounding into my own head over and over again.

For four days straight, she and I talked over the phone without him knowing. For six days, I laughed, went sightseeing and enjoyed my vacation, knowing this was going to be our last. By this time, he had completely turned his phone off or just left it in the hotel.

In those four days, the pieces of the puzzle started to come together.

I called his job and found out that his position in the company did not travel as he has quite a bit of vacation days. I relayed this information to "The Wife" who was in total shock. I wondered how for so long she couldn't know this. What wife doesn't know that her husband's job involves no travel whatsoever? How the tables turned in my mind.

I asked the wife in a rather snappy manner on the fourth day why she didn't leave him. What she told me elevated my power to infinity and made me realize how worthy I truly am. In a rather boastful way, like she was so proud of her position, she said, "All of you want to be the wife. I am the wife!"

I had to educate her that we are no longer in the fifties, and I prayed that she'd one day find her self-worth.

I found out during the week that every night at nine o'clock they video chatted. I was told he had a conference call for work. He duped and lied to both of us.

"The Wife" then sent me pictures of them vacationing for the three weeks he told me he was on a business trip, which led to both of us wondering where he was for the other two weeks.

I found out that the missing red BMW was actually her car. That weekend, she came into Orlando and left it at the airport where he picked it up.

She had no idea he had moved out of his condo as she stayed in Tampa or much less that he rented the four-bedroom house that we were supposed to live together in when we returned. I wondered what kind of wife did not know where her husband lived. She adamantly said the text messages regarding a divorce were not her messages. According to her, they never discussed divorce.

Oh, the sleepless nights, with slow, violent harmful thoughts I had as I stared at him sleeping. But God blessed me with children who needed a mother, plus I'm way too cute for jail. It takes an enormous amount of will to smile every day with all his lies quickly unraveling.

I had this brilliant plan of action. Take the sim card out of his phone and place it in my phone. Well, you know the saying "Be careful of what you might find when you go looking for stuff." Mind-blowing is an understatement!

Every holiday he gave us the same exact gift and flowers, and although my bouquets were much bigger, we received the same jewelry and perfumes. He had some damn nerve! This was a strategically, well-planned, type of cheating.

But wait, who was the other woman in the pictures smiling with her flowers on Valentine's day? I couldn't believe what my eyes were seeing, and, more importantly, I deeply hated myself because of my actions. Who was I becoming? This isn't my character. What happened to the woman who would simply walk away? Where did she go?

LOVE—that emotion called love—can put people in an unspeakable, dark place mentally. In less than six months, this was over-the-edge and too much. I was spiraling out of control. I was dealing with grief both from the loss of my grandmother and the loss of the man I thought I knew. Who wouldn't be grieving, honestly speaking?

Unless you're in this exact situation, there is no telling how you would react. That's the truth.

I wanted to send "The Wife" the pictures of the other woman, but what good would come out of that? They have kids. Instead, I told her what day, gate, and the time she could pick up her husband from the airport. She could have him!

Right then, I felt my love and respect for him leave my body. I was numb. Just when I felt liberated with the truth, who pops up in my message box on day five, but the "Other

Wife" Okay. Take a breath. It's okay to throw the book down and scream "The what!"

Yes, you read that right. He had two wives. At this point, my brain had reached its peak. I vomited and fainted. I kept in mind that he still remained clueless that I had been speaking with, shall we say, "The Main Wife," since she had been his wife the longest. As far as he was concerned, something I ate didn't agree with me.

I was having a full-blown text conversation with wife number two, who, by the way, was suing him for bigamy! She was the wife in the text messages regarding their divorce. Lord Jesus, take the wheel.

I'm learning that they honeymooned on St. Thomas, my beloved hometown. I'm thinking how on earth does "The Main Wife" not know about wife number two, plus me, and how could she be more naive than me? How did this become an episode of "Yas and her pitiful love life?"

I told "The Main Wife" about wife number two. She said that she knew! In fact, she bailed him out when he was arrested for bigamy. Her impression, however, was that the state dropped the charges and the other marriage was nullified and voided.

In my mind, I was thinking this man married another woman, and she is still claiming the "Wife" title? There is no dick on earth that good!

More lies surfaced. The court case he told me was the child support case that later turned into the divorce was actually the bigamy charge! Say that three times fast!

This man's blood is fueled by deceitfulness. His bone marrow is nothing more than unfiltered lies. It takes a special kind of mentality to emotionally have three women at the same time.

In this unbelievable, unbeknownst world of mine, the man I loved had "The Main Wife" in Tampa while the "Other Wife" was in Virginia and I, the clueless one, was in Orlando.

How could he emotionally find the time? I'm the one he was physically with the majority of the time.

Day seven finally arrived. By this point, I had a real nasty attitude as I should. He blamed me for destroying our getaway time with my coldness and called me selfish numerous times during the day, I stood and took all his harsh words and said nothing.

I knew on the other end of our flight from New York to Orlando would be a very pissed off, potty-mouth woman, "The Main Wife," in baggage claim waiting for her disgusting, no-good husband.

There was no need for me to lose another wasted emotion or my power. Freedom was on the horizon for me!

We walked off the plane toward baggage claim. I walked fast, almost in a jog. I could hear him telling me to slow down. Keep in mind, I had no idea the state of mind "The Main Wife" was in and I was not sticking around to find out.

Right before I dashed into the women's bathroom, I yelled to him. As I waved air quotes, I said, "Your wife is over there to pick up your sorry ass!"

As I made a mad dash for the very last stall, I heard some loud lady screaming and cursing. I thought, yes, she needs to give it to him and embarrass him! It's good for him!

I don't recall how long I stayed in that bathroom, but it had to be a good while as my bags were on the side in front of the office where you declare your lost luggage. I was not scared of her. I'd just had enough drama for an entire tribe of women.

I sorrowfully walked to the car. The reality was slowly setting in. The entire forty-five-minute drive, I cried and cried, mostly replaying her cruel words to me. You know the ones—bitch, whore, slut, homewrecker, and dumb shit.

Every day that passed, I sunk deeper inward. Beating myself up, I replayed the entire relationship over and over, I tried to fill in the gaps of the things I missed and how I missed them. My kids at this point took care of themselves as I could barely stand because my legs were so weak.

I couldn't eat or sleep, and I cried and hated myself more every day.

Men don't sit and think about the emotional damage and consequences of their selfish misdeeds. They probably think we are so resilient that we can bounce back from anything. For God's sake, we birth children and survive childbirth; we are warriors! I actually had a man tell me those exact words as to his rationale of why men hurt us emotionally.

What I'd been through wasn't only hurt. It was:

Ten tons of lies.

Forty cement trucks of betrayal.

Fifteen cruise ships of not give a shit about my body, my mind nor my soul.

It was one hundred thousand buried graves of grief.

An entire continent of African clay boulders dumbed on my head.

It was next level hurt. Like for real, let's really think about this. How many women reading this thought, oh my gosh, I can relate?

After two entire months of being in this state, my neighbor John happened to pick up my daughter walking home from school. I'm guessing she said something to him of my condition. There he was at the foot of my bed yelling at me to go take a bath. I don't recall if I had been bathing. Maybe I smelled. I don't know, and I doubt that I cared, honestly.

As I dragged my ugly crying, ugly feeling self into the shower, John said to me, "Woman, this looks like depression."

Now, let's roll all the way back to *Journey Untold - Twisted Love—My Mother's Struggle with Mental Illness*. I stood there frozen in time, looking at myself in the mirror and thinking, *Oh, my God, I am my mother*! My entire life I swore to myself that I would never become my mother.

This all happened before I wrote my Journey Untold and found compassion for my mother's illness. Being my mother was the ultimate, worst thing ever in life to be!

I must have had a come to Jesus moment as I ran to my phone and searched for my therapist's phone number. I had completely forgotten that there was a man in my bathroom who had never seen me in my birthday suit. I called her and adamantly told her that I needed to see her as soon as possible. I told her I was depressed, and I didn't want to be depressed anymore!

If you know me personally, you know that my freak out moments involve me speaking really fast and ranting over and over again about the same thing for a good half hour. Since my Florida therapist had been my therapist since my divorce, she knew this was a siren-blowing moment.

The next day, she was at my door. I don't play with my mental health. Just as if I'd known that my mother died of breast cancer, I'd take precautionary measures to prevent cancer. My mother had a mental illness, so heck, yes, I was going to take precautionary measures to prevent the onset of mental illness.

I was not diagnosed with depression. What I had been through, my brain had said enough, I'm done, peace out, I quit, screw this shit and took a damn time out. Flag on the play!

She encouraged me to start from day-one when he and I met. As you can imagine, this was extremely difficult to do. It was necessary for my healing. For one day, every week for six months, I cried and healed. I was no longer his victim in this twisted plot. I survived and conquered. This is what talk therapy does. It heals you from the inside out while chopping away all that dead skin, so you can have that earthly sun-kissed glow.

We celebrated the last day of therapy knowing that it would be the last time I would see her. I was happy to know I was going to be okay; bittersweet, nonetheless.

I was back to myself and never skipped a beat from my regular Facebook posts. Yet, no one outside of my close circle knew that my kids and I were steadily trying to cope daily.

The next six months I found that my clothing line had evolved into something amazing. My, how God puts you through challenges only to have your wings clipped, but also to prepare you for the flight ahead. I didn't date, I didn't text, nor did I call a single man. I was focused on my kids and my clothing line. That was my happy place. I can honestly tell you that trusting a man was nonexistent during this time. It was so bad that trust packed up his shit and moved into the black hole.

I did hear from him again. He tried to sue me for my clothing line but failed. After I wrote the first book, he sent me a message on my Facebook business page saying how proud he was of me. He said that he was going to be in Orlando and would love to treat me to dinner.

I said sure, and even setup the place and time. For all I know, he is still there waiting as I never showed. The block feature and I formed our first close bond.

Over a year passed, and I knew that to move forward and not allow what this one man did to me affect me being loved and giving love, I had to start dating again.

Know that if you mention the word Match, my anxiety would twitch. Instead, I tried a different app. My thoughts were "Oh, the men on this app must be better!" Duh, it's the app, of course.

The second day on the app, a handsome guy sent me a message. I asked him what he was doing. He said, "Watching basketball." I said, "Let's go to the beach." With a little hesitation, he did meet me on the beach.

Now you're probably thinking, Yas, you are not thinking right, but I was. Have you ever seen an empty beach in Florida in the middle of summer? Nope! The restaurant was so loud we could barely hear each other. Honestly, I just wanted company and to push past my fear. Step one complete.

Going to the beach was different for him. Over time, about two weeks into our dating, I felt that he became emotionally in-tune with me. He was slowly growing on me. After a month of getting to know him, he asked me to go to Miami to celebrate his friend's fiftieth birthday on a yacht. I was dying to get away, so I said, "Heck, yeah, let's go!"

I dropped the kids off with their godmother, and to the water and yacht, we went. I was in an I can tolerate him, he's cool to be around, he is funny and let's see where this goes phase.

I had an amazing time on the yacht and went to sleep thinking I wouldn't mind getting to know him better. But I woke up to him looking over me like, "Uh oh, I'm so sorry, Yas!"

Still groggy as I'm not a morning person at all, I asked him, "What happened? What did you do?"

He said, "I put us in a relationship on Facebook, and all these people started commenting."

You see, he was not keen to know how Facebook works.

My internal voice said, *Noooo*!!!!! My loud voice said, "What on earth have you done!"

Frantically, I took his phone. Hundreds of congratulations were popping up, and I thought, my Lord, make this nightmare stop. I went to check my inbox to see if the wife sent me a message. Not that he had one, but I thought this way because of my last relationship.

Embarrassed and thinking great, since the entire world knows, let's do this.

I found myself posting kissing and hugging pictures. Life was moving forward again, or so I thought.

Since the end of the last relationship, I gained a new circle of friends. One woman, I nicknamed the "FBI." If this guy was married, she would find his divorce papers. She found his marriage license but no divorce papers.

The minute she told me, I confronted him. What happened next?

Here I was again, in a Facebook relationship with a legally married man in which I had met his brother, his mother, and his kids. How could this be my life?

He told me that he signed the papers and gave them to his ex-wife to file, and she didn't follow through. At this point, my emotions put up her two fingers and said "deuces." Again, I was back in the "trust for no man" black hole. So, I told him let's go to the courthouse and file these papers. We filled them out, made an appointment, sat down and waited for his number to be called. When his number was called to pay, he couldn't go through with it.

He said that he was not ready for his marriage to be over.

Since I had already emotionally checked out, I said, "It's been real; I'm out." Then, I left him right there in the courthouse.

Through therapy, I gained the power to not allow circumstances to dominate my emotions.

One day, he showed up at my job and apologized. Today, we are still friends, and he is still on my Facebook page. I see him liking and commenting every day. I've never asked nor cared if he went back to his wife or divorced. We joke about me going to bed single and waking up in a relationship, as it's now hilarious.

I stayed single for pretty much the remainder of my time in Orlando until I moved to Georgia. I needed to hit the reset button.

Chapter Nine: Engaged to a Narcissist

Narcissism is a mental condition; a disorder in which a person has an inflated sense of self-importance. Narcissistic personality disorder is found more commonly in men. The cause is unknown, but it likely involves a combination of genetic and environmental factors.

Narcissists have a grandiose sense of self-importance and live in a fantasy world that supports their delusions of grandeur. They need constant praise and admiration and have a sense of entitlement. They also exploit others without guilt or shame, and frequently demean, intimidate, bully, or belittle others. But, behind this mask of extreme confidence, lies a fragile low self-esteem that's vulnerable to the slightest criticism.

Speaking from my experience, love from a narcissist can leave the other person emotionally hurt and terribly confused. Unless you have experienced the behavior of a narcissist up close and personal, you won't see them coming. They don't have personalities that switch from time-to-time.

Narcissists camouflage their true self. In my case, he had me believing that he had every important trait of a man that

I've waited on all my life until his representative could not hide any longer and showed up one day.

Narcissists typically don't see themselves as such. In fact, they are one hundred percent perfect. Even if you're standing in front of them bewildered, hurt and in a state of instant confusion, they think the victim of their emotional backlash is at fault for everything that went wrong in the relationship.

I waited two years to grow, settle in, establish my business roots and learn my way around Georgia. I'm a believer that all things happen for a reason as well as I'm not going to block my blessings in front of me.

In those two years, I went out on dates but nothing serious. Most connections did not last past a week. I didn't meet anyone who seriously knew what they wanted and were ready to date seriously. Hopeful and optimistic, I continued to date in my free time.

In early spring 2017, I received a message on the dating app from an older guy who looked great for his age. Skeptical at that point in my life, I had no desire or interest in older men. Honestly, I felt older men could not possibly keep up with me and my busy business life. Dating men in their forties were already challenging, so I couldn't envision a man over fifty.

It's amazing how we analyze scenarios in our minds without ever experiencing them.

With nothing but time to lose, I responded. It was one of the best text conversations that had any real substance. He followed the ask and answer rhythm. As he answered one of my questions, he would then ask a question. This continued for a week.

Intrigued with our text conversations, we agreed to exchange numbers. Speaking with him was a complete delight. His laugh was infectious, and the conversations were stimulating.

He was interested in my life and showed great interest in the type and sort of man I needed. He did not boast or brag about himself. He just wanted to learn about my interests and about me. This was different and unique compared to any man I'd met before. Imagine a world where someone is generally interested in you and put in the effort to build a friendship together. I felt like I'd hit the man lottery! He was handsome, a great conversationalist, funny, witty, successful, and knew what he wanted in a woman—and it was me.

He asked me out for our first date. It was a Friday night at nine. He was a gentleman and met me at my car in the parking lot. I remember this so clearly as it was one of the best dates, I'd had in quite some time. It was truly refreshing. We talked, laughed, and ate good food. He asked many more questions about the characteristics and the type of man I was looking for.

I kind of felt like I was on a man-inquisition or interview. I've never experienced this type of questioning before. Naive yet intrigued and giggling, I answered.

For example: Are you the type of woman who likes a man to open the car door each time?

Would you like it better if a man calls you or do you prefer text messages?

Do you like a man who's thoughtful and buys you gifts?

These questions seem normal, right? This is what you would like to have men ask when getting to know you. There were two straight hours of questions with the same rhythm: asks and answer.

In hindsight, for every answer I gave him, somehow, he began morphing into a man who matched my answers.

Right before we were told by our waitress that the restaurant was about to close, he did something I was simply wasn't ready or prepared for. He grabbed his phone and told me, "If I'm serious about dating, let's both get off the app and truly get to know each other." Those words made my ears tingle from the eardrum all the way down to my earrings. It sounded magical and felt like the tunes of the sweet sounds of jazz to my delicate ears. I've but only dreamed of a man taking charge of knowing what he wants, and I found it. Inside, I screamed, *finally!*

He called to make sure I made it home safely and said he couldn't wait to spend time with me again. He invited me to a barbeque at his friend's house the following Sunday and asked if I would like to attend Jamaican Jerk Fest with him. That gesture made me smile.

I felt so special that he wanted to introduce me to his friends. Embracing my culture is also important to me; it shows that he was open-minded to new things, and I didn't have to ask.

Not remembering at that moment, I did mention that it would be nice if the man for me was interested and open-minded about Caribbean culture.

I counted down the minutes and seconds until my eyes could gaze into his beautiful, glossy, brown eyes and I could hear his loud, tantalizing laugh.

As he walked outside, every step he took was in slow motion. As he opened my passenger door, I could smell his cologne. I thought, Good Lord, he smells so good!

The smile on his face as he looked at me made my heart flutter. He turned up the music in his car and we were dancing and singing on the way. We were in a zone of happyville.

At the barbeque, he could not take his hands off me. It was so cute!

It felt fantastic to be wanted in this manner of love. For years, I've only dreamed of feeling like this. Many nights I've laid on my bed staring at the ceiling envisioning this is what being in love would look and feel like.

All of his friends commented how happy we looked. My face was flushed from blushing.

We left the barbeque and headed to the Jerk Fest. On the way, the song, "I Just Want to be Happy" came on, and he sang it to me. I chimed in and recorded it on Instagram. To see someone as happy as he felt amazing. My dream is to add joy to someone's life and vice versa. It felt safe to start liking him. Just living in the moment and letting God guide us. He liked me, and I liked him. The connection felt real!

At the festival, we danced until the music stopped. Oh, the fun we had. He was such a people person. With everyone around us, he would strike up a joyful conversation. My cheeks hurt from smiling and laughing the entire night.

During the drive home, I wished time would stop so I could take in every amazing, blissful feeling I was having. If this was just the start of the relationship, bring on the months and years to come, I thought.

A month later, my daughter wanted her mom-time at the lake. I told him that I needed to spend time with her. He asked if she would mind if he came along. My throat felt like I'd swallowed an acorn. What! I'm very protective of her and unless I'm comfortable with anyone of the other sex, they will not grace her presence.

Then he said, "I can bring the barbeque grill and cook for you." I think he saw the scared look on my face and said this to soften the blow. I consulted with my daughter to see if she would even entertain the idea of sharing her mom-time with someone.

As I reflect back, he must have really made an impact for me to even consider the idea. Normally, my answer would be hell no!

She was okay with the idea of him coming along to cook, but he had to drive his own car. You see, this was her mom and daughter time. I told her my friend was coming to cook on the grill.

He was actually cool with it. Inside, I thought, he isn't offended? I took it as a gesture of him being respectful of her, compassionate and understanding that this was her time. Major brownie points!

My daughter and I were at the lake an hour by ourselves. He came later and set up the barbeque.

Since my daughter loves to cook, I felt this would be a good bonding moment. His food was absolutely finger-licking good. I also mentioned in one of our conversations that cooking was one of her loves.

All that time, I was thinking, "Wow, God sent me the most attentive man ever with a keen ability to pick up on details that matter to me."

During the week, we talked for hours. Sometimes, if he completed his work shift early, we would go to the gym and work out or go out to dinner. I would count the minutes and seconds until I got to spend time with him again.

I looked forward to our weekends together as if I were back in high school and giddy, falling fast and strong. We went somewhere every Saturday and Sunday. He was a truck driver, so it was his time to live. It was just him, me, and my daughter.

It was the start of the fourth quarter for my thriving Amazon business as orders were pouring in. Without me asking, he came over on many occasions to help pack orders.

What! I struck gold in a man with all the characteristics I admire, and he was willing to help me with my business! Yeah, God, I thank you.

My emotions were becoming deeper and deeper. From day one, I've always been involved with his photography business. After one week of dating him, he scheduled a photo shoot to show me his skills. He does, in fact, have a great eye! After gracing many magazine covers, I was even more impressed. I believed in all of him. Wanting to be there to see him succeed and watching him work turned me on as he was so sexy and passionate about his skills.

Things were going smoothly. I wanted to pinch myself, but I didn't want to wake up if this was just a dream. Nobody could touch the cloud nine I was on.

The following month, I met his daughter and ex-wife at his house. They were both delightful. His ex-wife and I became good friends instantly. She signed up to become one of my BOSS students.

We enjoyed going to lunch, and, of course, shopping. Others would be amazed by our friendship, but it didn't bother us. Our friendship had nothing to do with him.

However, once I met them, his demeanor changed a bit. It was rather sudden and took me for a tailspin. He stopped being affectionate. The hugging stopped. There were no more hugs when he came to pick me up or when we greeted each other. We also didn't hug around his friends. We would only hug when watching a movie. When we would spend the night at each other's home, he would roll over and turn his back to me. I made up so many excuses and scenarios in my mind.

He was tired, and I would be tired too if I drove all week. I needed to be understanding and compassionate.

He has a lot on his mind.

Maybe it's me? Something must be wrong with me?

Maybe I said or did something wrong?

The mind starts coming to its own conclusions as to what's wrong. It has to be me. What else could it be?

One day, I invited him to go for a walk in the park to talk. I felt uncomfortable having this conversation at either of our homes as both of our girls lived with us.

As we walked through the peacefulness of nature, I asked him point blank, "Why have you stopped hugging me?"

Looking straight in my face, he said, "I'm not a hugger. I never hugged you!" Then, he called his female cousin on the phone and asked her "if he was the hugging type?" She said, "No," in a surprised tone, as if it to inquire if that was the real reason for his call.

TRIANGULATION

It is a vicious tactic of bringing a third person in the picture or another perspective in order to validate their actions while invalidating your thoughts.

Triangulation is a horrible way of manipulating someone's thoughts by making them suspect their own sanity. The person who is brought to validate their actions is often someone from their closest circle, or in the worst case, another tricked individual.

This mind game proceeds as they defend their behavior and use the third-party as a weapon against your uncertainties until you've completely lost your sanity.

GASLIGHTING

A narcissist's most cunning manipulative tactic is convincing you that you are actually imagining things and that you are crazy. Gas-lighting is a method used to escape accountability for their actions.

How it works:

By slowly distorting a person's sense of reality, gas-lighting affects their moral sense of separating right from wrong, which can eventually end up with the person losing the ability to trust their own conscience. Through gas-lighting, a narcissist may confuse the person. They can twist the truth often and constantly insist that the person is remembering things differently.

I questioned myself, my thoughts, memory, and even my own sanity. He made me feel that I could not rely on my own thoughts and should only trust what he was saying. I felt like I'd walked into a different parallel universe. I stood there thinking, maybe he really never hugged me after all?

I played the videos of us hugging each other over and over and thought that when he said it was dancing, that's what it was—dancing. He was correct. He wasn't hugging me; he was just guiding me through the crowd. When I showed those same videos to him, that was his rationale.

Gas-lighting, in my opinion, is mental brainwashing. The sad part is that I couldn't see this is what he was a master of, regardless of my exposure and training in mental health.

Every day I wondered what happened and secretly hoped that he'd come back to give me the biggest hug and apologize.

Clinging to hope, I remained desperate. I knew that his hugging me was not a figment of my imagination. But I didn't have anyone in my corner to call and tell him that they had also seen him hugging me and to stop playing games.

Inside, my thoughts were strongly urging me to run away from him. Yet, love kept me there, remembering every single time he held me close.

A narcissist may start their wicked game by taking you way up in love and idealizing you until you're all hooked and addicted to their "perfect "personality. That's what happened to me. I fell in love with him, and he knew it. The moment he realized it, things started to change, and I couldn't see it clearly.

In late November, he started spending his money on things he didn't need. Since we weren't married or engaged, I turned a blind eye but took notes, of course.

At some point, he was a good twenty thousand dollars in debt. My business mind can't fathom spending money and not getting a return on the investment.

He was lying on his bed as I reached the point of not being able to hold my tongue any longer. I shared my concerns about his rapid spending habits and lack of affection. What he said to me really prepared me to start mentally checking out of this relationship.

The words: "I'll add this to my list!"

My internal self said, *hold up, this man is really putting my needs and concerns on a Goddamn list*! *Oh, no, he didn't*!

My body stood still in shock for at least a good twenty minutes or so. Yet, I said nothing. You see, my internal voice was screaming inside, spurring thoughts of, Yas, tell this fool you're out! Put up your deuces and bounce!

The only thing I can recall saying was, "Oh, okay, we are making a checklist of emotions now! I got you!" Then, I calmly left his house.

I did not react the entire fifteen-minute drive back to my house. If I can explain in words, I felt like two separate people toggling between letting my inner thoughts out and standing up to this nonsense or just checking out completely with a big fat *next*.

Instead of getting angry, I felt that he *would always* think he was right and make me feel like I was crazy, and what I thought I was seeing, or witnessing was all "in my head." What was the point in speaking to him?

He called and texted for hours, and for the first time, I completely ignored him. The more I ignored him, the more aggressive he became, and he eventually showed up in my driveway.

I refused to move off my bed. Instead, I texted him, "It's not on my list to come to the door." That's when he realized that I still had power in myself, and his insecurity showed full blown.

He inserted the blame game and said this was all my fault and that I wanted to change him and found fault in everything. He went as far as to argue with me about cleaning his house!

Thank God, I had my own house, my daughter, and my work to help channel my internal outrage.

One thing I can say about him is that he does not stay mad for long. It's like the incident never happened, and he was back to laughing and making jokes.

Although he never apologized, he fell back into being affectionate. This time, he even turned it up a notch. He said he really wanted to spend his life with me by his side and would do everything to love me the way I deserved. I saw the devotion in his eyes, and I could feel the commitment in the way he touched me.

Unbeknownst to me, he was what I considered to be brainwashing.

BRAINWASHING

Have you ever ended up doing things you didn't feel comfortable doing just for the sake of the other person? You feel that if you don't do the things they ask, you've failed them, and you feel guilty for not performing the way you should.

He shamed me in front of everyone and called it a joke. Yes, in front of others, he joked about our first argument. I laughed as well, but deep inside, I was appalled that he brought up our personal life to others and that I was the blunt of his jokes. There's no way I could have a normal dialog with him. I questioned myself whether I could live with him for the rest of my life and then I turned around and looked at his current actions.

Anytime the conversation would be about Amazon and my success, he would take over the conversation and start bragging about his photography to the point he would go in the car for his laptop. He would start showing pictures, and everyone would tell him how great his photos are.

I'm quite secure in myself and will happily step aside and let another person shine. I'm the type who will sit and applaud your greatness alongside everyone else.

My lease was coming to an end, and I was toggling between buying a new home or renting a bigger house as my businesses were expanding.

I mentioned my options to him but not for him to find any sort of solutions. I honestly just wanted to have a conversation. Maybe if I heard my own voice, then I'd find my own way.

In an instant, he invited us to move in with him. My response was pure confusion. How, out of that conversation, did he get that we needed to come and live with him?

My mind instantly went to my daughter. I was scared. Since my divorce, we have not lived with others. Can we even cohabitate with others?

I told him that I didn't think that would be a good example for my daughter. It's not okay for me to live with a man and not be married. Surprisingly, he agreed.

The following weekend, in front of my daughter, he proposed. I didn't have a chance to say yes. Let me explain. At the time, I thought this was funny. The one thing our relationship had was laughter. That's what kept us whole.

We took my daughter to the mall to shop for her friends, brothers and her dad's Christmas gifts. Whenever we went to a mall, he would always stop to look at Citizen watches.

This day was no different. I joked and told him we would be over in the area looking for rings.

My daughter and I were messing with the salesclerk, trying on rings. It was more fun for us than looking at watches, yet again.

The manager came out and offered one of the rings to us at half the sticker price. I declined and said we weren't actually looking for rings and noted that my boyfriend was on the other side looking at watches.

To our surprise, he said he would throw in a two-thousand-dollar Citizen watch for free.

He didn't flinch and handed the manager his card. Walla, I was engaged. My daughter was shocked by what happened, and so was I. I started to laugh because I honestly felt it must be a joke!

In what should have been my moment, he was jumping up and down happy for the free watch. This time, I finally felt brave enough to tell him just how wrong this was and handed him back the ring.

That same week, on Thursday, he called and told me to dress nicely as he was taking me out to dinner. He took me to Chateau Elan. It's not unusual for him to call and ask me out to dinner. We did that three to four days a week.

We arrived, and everything seemed normal. We talked, laughed, and ate our food. Little did I know he made arrangements with the server, who walked up to me and told me when I went to the restroom earlier that I dropped something. I'm always dropping or forgetting something.

I got up to look around, and when I turned back around, looking confused, he was on his knees with the ring. I said, "Yes," followed by, "but there are some things that we need to discuss." He agreed. We had a very lovely dinner. The night ended perfectly.

Still leery about moving in, I spoke to my attorney about my concerns. He suggested that we sign a living-in agreement. This is similar to a lease, except it states in detail exactly what my role and responsibilities would be while living in his house.

It stated what my financial responsibility would be. It was an open agreement that protected my daughter and me. I just didn't feel comfortable and ready to live with him. This agreement was for six months. I was free to leave if I chose to and did not owe him any money if I left. We both agreed and signed it.

All of my fears were covered, and he could not throw us out if he pleased or try to sue me for money. Here I was, donating and selling everything I owned for the last twenty-three years of my life in America. The dining-room table was the hardest piece of furniture for me to get rid of. I cried as it went through the door. All four of my children spent time laughing and bonding while eating at that table. I convinced myself that it was time for something new.

I was in total delight and open-minded to almost everything. I was also happy that I was gaining another wonderful daughter and that the man of my dreams had returned and that hope in us was restored. We were one beautiful, happy family.

He often discussed his cousin who was like a brother to him. When he spoke about this particular cousin, I could hear the emotion in his voice. They were extremely close. I'd often wondered if he was close to his family. Outside of his children, ex-wife, a female cousin in California and a male cousin in Carolina, I didn't hear him speak on the phone to anyone else.

When I would ask about his other family members, he was rather short, especially about the relationship between him and his mother.

He expressed that night on the drive home that he could not wait to share his exciting engagement news. His ex-wife and children, who often told me that it was great to see their dad so happy, were very glad for him.

While driving, the next day after our engagement, his phone rang. The person on the phone asked him what he was doing. He told them where we were going and that he was driving. My world with him changed after this phone call.

The person told him to stop and pull over, which he did. The words I caught were, "Your brother was murdered. It looks like someone tried to rob him," and "There was blood everywhere."

My heart hurt deeply for him. I never met his brother, and yet I had tears falling from my eyes.

What he said to me hurt my soul. He said, "I'll never get a chance to tell him I'm engaged," and "How can he be dead!" He showed no remorse. I'm very understanding that people grieve differently, but his demeanor was subzero.

I've never seen this type of behavior in my life. No sadness, no nothing. What transpired next was even more of a shock. He picked up the phone and started calling everyone he knew. It was like a scene out of a movie.

He turned his brother's death into a sympathy cry for himself. Instead of having others mourn for the loss of their relative, he made them mourn for him.

His voice would quiver as he told them the news. Each time he told them about the way his brother died, the version became twisted into another unspoken reality. You would think he was actually there.

He told one of his cousins in a somber way and said he was brutally murdered at a bar. Then he screamed sadly and said, "I can't believe he's dead." He didn't have to die this way. He told stories of when they were younger, followed by he wasn't sure he was going to make it through this.

All his family members fed into his mind trap and started crying for him and telling him how sorry they were for his loss.

I'm sitting in the driver's seat looking at him and asking myself if I had walked into the twilight zone. Do they not realize this is *all* of their loss? Did I jump from the moving car and miss the part about the bar? Who lies on the dead for self-gratification?

After he made all his calls, the new version ended up with him being too drunk when he left the bar, and someone followed him home and killed him in his house, leaving him to die.

What really happened to his brother? He had stage four cancer and refused care. The blood all over him was from his vomiting and complications from cancer.

My only thoughts were, Lord, don't you leave me to die in front of this man because I have no idea what the story of my death will be. I was completely dumbfounded.

Outside of the phony, emotional act on the phone, he appeared scary-normal around me. He started doing his laundry and cleaning his room.

I said to him, "If you need a shoulder to cry on, know that I'm here. He snapped at me and said, "I don't cry!"

For the duration of his grieving and making plans to travel, I stayed close to my daughter. We went out and did things together. I did not want her to witness this type of grief. This was not the norm for me. It was so unbelievable that I slept in my office. At one point, he told me that I was to drive up with him, but all the while, I didn't want to go. I already felt ostracized and excluded completely, right here in Georgia. I didn't need to go to another state and feel even more like I didn't belong. I also didn't think this was the way his family should meet his new fiancé because this was not a time to celebrate. Needless to say, I was relieved when he told me to stay.

For a couple of days after he returned from the funeral, he walked around somberly and would sit and rub his head. After that, he was back to cracking jokes and laughing as if nothing ever happened.

I started to feel like this was not where I wanted to be and questioned if I really wanted to be with this man for the rest of my life. The moment you question yourself, you already know the answer. I didn't want to face my own truth, at least not yet.

How cold would it have been if, in his time of grief, I had left? So, I stayed because a fiancé is supposed to be with you through the good and bad times, right? You can't be with the person only in their good times; you need to be there for them at their lowest times. That's how I convinced myself to stay.

Just a few days later, he sat me down and discussed his estranged relationship with his mom. He told me that earlier in the day he was told she had stage four cancer. His cousins planned a road trip to go see her.

I prayed for him as there was nothing else I could do. This was a lot for him to handle, and it wasn't even Christmas yet.

I can tell you first-hand that he does not handle bad news or grief well. It changed him. He was cold, attention-seeking and in a deep, self-preservation mode.

We all mentioned to him that maybe he should see someone just to talk things out. He refused and didn't think he needed help.

January came and went. I was trying to hold on emotionally. He coped by putting all his focus on his photography and spending more money on things he didn't need. I was happy that he was happy.

Valentine's Day rolled around, and after kissing me on my forehead, he didn't even give me a Happy Valentine's Day gift when he left for work. This man gave gifts and love most of the time. He didn't need a reason, and that's why I was shocked on this day.

He came home to my gifts and enjoyed them greatly. He said he had to go put gas in his car and that he would be right back. He returned with a huge box of chocolates for the girls and three cacti for me.

I know you're thinking, "Wait, did she say three cacti," as in plants?" "*Yes!*"

I wanted to scream. Who the hell buys a woman a damn cactus, especially on Valentine's Day! What was he trying to say, exactly? That I'm a prick!

Yet, I said, "Thank you, this is different!" What do you say that's nice to something like this?

March, April, and May went by, and we didn't see much of each other. This time of year is devoted to my daughter and keeping her comfortable, calm, and focused in school with back-to-back standardized tests. Plus, it's my Amazon business busy season.

For the third year, we were getting ready for a summer cruise with the Royal Vision Voyage annual empowerment cruise in which I am a speaker. This would be the first time he and I would travel together, and it was a good test of our relationship and way for me to decide whether to stay or go.

He was excited, but not for the same reason I was. I was excited to spend quality time with him. He was excited to take his thousand dollars of photo equipment on the cruise.

In my life, there is this one girlfriend I have in Florida who can tell from my posts that she needs to pick up the phone and call me.

She is also one of those friends who understands entrepreneurship. She knows I love her even though we can go months without speaking. We can pick right back up from where we left off and spend hours on one phone call to catch up until the next time.

I told her everything. She asked me very specific questions and told me to look up narcissist. I put her on speaker and then started to Google. Every word I read sounded just like him. These stories from other women sounded like my own. But how did I miss this, I thought. How could I be a mental health advocate and completely miss this?

She told me that's because he gas-lighted me, and that unless I had met one, then I wouldn't know.

I was obsessed with the internet as I was closer to getting answers about his behavior that had me in total confusion.

At that moment, I told myself not to betray my self-worth, especially for a relationship!

I picked up the phone and asked his ex-wife, my good friend, to accompany me to dinner. We never spoke about him. Now, I needed to.

At dinner, I expressed that I respected her as his ex-wife and mother of his children. I didn't want her to break any codes nor did I want this to be about us bad-mouthing him. I needed someone who, at that moment, might be able to relate to how I was feeling. She listened. She didn't need to say a single word as her facial expressions were confirmation.

When I asked, "How did you cope for so long?" Her response was that she focused on raising the children.

As we were about to go our separate ways, she hugged me and told me to just enjoy the cruise. And, whatever I did, to not lose myself, and after the cruise, decide what I was going to do.

Unbeknownst to me, the Lord knew that I needed to hear this message. Her words kept me whole.

We had a fabulous time on the cruise. There was one moment I was in utter astonishment, and that slowly showed me the exit door.

I can't swim, and yet that does not stop me from diving off boats, snorkeling and engaging in other water activities. As long as there is a life jacket and someone who can swim around me, I'm covered.

One of the excursions was swimming with the stingrays, which I could not wait to do! My Tampa girlfriend, who is more like a sister to me and a second mom to my daughter, came along on this trip.

Everyone in our group knew I couldn't swim. The boat had to dock in deep water and then we would have to swim to the reef.

In front of him, my girlfriend asked me if I needed her to help me. He said, "No, she is fine."

Both my daughter and my girlfriend, who are strong swimmers, left without me but continued to look back. They are very protective of me, and it's instinctive for them to know if I'm okay.

He jumped off the boat and then I jumped off the boat, thinking he was ready to catch me. Instead of catching me, he swam away, and I didn't have on a life vest!

Now, all eyes were on me struggling to stay above the water. I could see my girlfriend and my daughter rushing coming to save me.

My girlfriend was screaming at him and swimming at the same time.

I was on the reef safe and pissed! Everyone in our group was upset at him and asked why he didn't help me.

My girlfriend wanted to kill him, and my daughter was upset with him as she could not comprehend how he just swam off and left her mother.

He came over to me, not to apologize or accept responsibility, but to splash water on me like nothing ever happened.

I dunked his head underwater until he choked and asked him how it felt. I was that mad!

Our cruise ended. It was time to head back to reality.

When we arrived at our airport gate, they announced the plane was broken. My anxiety said, "I'm not flying on a broken plane!" They offered vouchers, and I mentioned to him that we should get them. He insisted that we waited to see what would happen.

Some six hours later sitting on hard seats, tired and hungry, they announced the flight was canceled. There was about twelve of us remaining. Even though we were tired, and by this point my daughter, who lives with autism, had completely mentally checked out. I was in my "thinking for her mode" as she could not think for herself. I couldn't get her to find her center and decided to just let her be. I'd take care of both of us. I was beyond exhausted, but I paid no attention to my self-care. So, I thought my child came first, and I'll take my time when I get back to Georgia.

But, when your mind and body has had enough, it will shut down.

We had our hotel vouchers and were instructed to leave the airport, go outside of the terminal and walk half a mile to catch a bus. The bus would take us to the hotel.

Until now, there has never been a time that this man let me carry my bags. I struggled with a garment bag that my daughter was supposed to carry, my backpack, and a carry-on. He only had on a backpack, and his hands were free.

I was getting angrier by the minute, but I had to put my anger aside and get my child to the hotel. That's how I was coping.

All of a sudden, I didn't feel well. I'd never felt that way before. I stopped and yelled at him that something was wrong with me. He turned and said, "just keep going." I was shaking, cold, then hot and I could feel the blood in my head pounding. My left arm went numb, and all of my fingers were tingling. The balls of my feet were tingling, and my vision was blurry.

Oh my God, what's happening, I thought. I could barely see my daughter, but I could see she was on the bench. I willed my body to take a step, then another and another. I was dragging the garment bag on the ground, but my fingers wanted so badly to let go of both bags. I wanted to drop to the ground and lie down.

I was finally sitting next to my daughter, who I could see was trapped in her own world. Her eyes were blank. She didn't look at me or move her head left or right. She was stoic. I felt sick and helpless for her and myself. Self-hate as a helpless mother crept in, and I didn't have time to process it, so my eyes decided to go inside of my head as I laid on my zombie daughter's lap.

Where was he? Two benches down as if he wasn't with us.

I can't recall when the bus arrived. I faintly heard my name called to get on the bus. I sat on someone in the front seat and then fell out. I could hear voices saying, "She doesn't look well."

I was alert again, and this time, I was sitting on a blue couch. I assumed I was in the hotel. Nothing made sense to me. I could hear everything all at once. My heart, blood pumping, footsteps, and people talking. My mouth was so parched that my lips felt like they were bleeding.

I heard someone yell out to me, "I need your ID."

I yelled back, "I need water!"

My eyes opened wide enough, and my vision improved just in time for me to watch him put his hands up in the air and utter these words in front of everyone: "I'm tired. I'm not dealing with her and this bullshit. Let's go, Misha."

Then, just like that, I felt as if my brain just gave up, and my body followed. I lost the fight to think or move. I thought I died; it felt like I died.

I fell unconscious. As my body shut down, I felt a hand on my left wrist. I heard her say she was a doctor, and my pulse was extremely weak and to call 911.

I was abruptly awakened by two male strangers in front of me. One was shining a light in my eyes, and another one was trying to force a liquid down my throat, telling me in a harsh manner to drink it.

Bottle after bottle, I'm swallowing whatever they were giving me.

"Mr. Flashlight," asked, if I had any allergies or high blood pressure. I felt like I was answering because I was telling him that I was allergic to penicillin, but the words weren't coming out of my mouth.

Someone said they thought I was with my daughter and asked the hotel clerk to call up to the room.

I saw my daughter; she was focused, alert and then I fainted. It was like my brain said, "Thank you, Jesus, she is okay, and then I fell asleep"

"Mr. Flashlight" was in front of me again trying to wake me. I looked over to my daughter, and she was talking to "Mr. Drink this."

I faintly heard her telling him the name of all my medications. My daughter pushed passed all of her struggles, such as her fear of talking to strangers. I'd never seen her be such an adult. In that short space of time, she went from being seventeen with autism to over forty and standing tall at the plate. She knew her mom needed her, and she saved my life.

All those trips to my doctor's office with me forcing her to come inside with me helped her to know my medical history. I knew there was a reason she had to know my entire medical history even though she felt grossed out and ridiculous about being there.

"Mr. Flashlight," asked me if I had eaten anything and if I had high blood pressure. I said no to both questions.

He told me in a very stern manner that my pressure was one hundred ninety over some number. I was stuck on the one hundred ninety and I didn't hear the other number. I knew that was dangerously high. His words that they needed to get me to a hospital rang in my head. I said, "My daughter has to come with me."

I was told she could take an Uber, but there was no room for her. Very stern and as alert as I could be, I said, "I'm not going anywhere without her! I'm not leaving her with him!"

You see, at that moment, I honestly felt he was the devil. I was terrified of the devil. I don't know if it was because of my blood pressure or my body, but in my mind, he really was the devil in human flesh.

The devil was out to kill me.

Since I refused to go to the hospital, they did all they could to lower my pressure. The same lady who held my hand was still there, this time rubbing my back.

I wish I had been strong enough to ask her for her name. I can't even remember her face.

More water to drink. I'm fully alert now. They checked my pressure, and it was down to one hundred seventy-five, still high.

I had to sign a waiver refusing care. My daughter couldn't sign because she was too young. They called him down.

As he arrived, he was acting like this caring, concerned husband to be, and started asking everyone what was wrong with me. I was still connected to the EKG machine. My mind was cursing. Oh now, you want to show up and pretend to freaking care. Go away from here! You good-for-nothing piece of shit! Scatter your demonic ass!

My mouth couldn't say a word of what I was thinking. The machine was just beeping out of control. The lady asked if he hits me. I said, "no," but "I'd surely like to take a lead pipe to his sorry ass! I said this very loudly!

I was instructed to breathe to balance my heart rate.

Now, the devil was touching me, escorting me in the elevator and to the room. In my mind, I'd recited every prayer of protection my granny had ever told me.

I was lying on the bed with my daughter. He was sitting on the edge of the other bed looking at me, just pitiful. I looked at my daughter, and said to her, "Any man who treats you this way and leaves you to die, you run," then I fell asleep holding her.

The time came to get up and catch our flight. He carried all the bags, but neither my daughter nor I said anything. My daughter was fully in charge of me. She made me eat something even though I didn't want to.

He tried to talk to her, and she told him, "Shut up and be quiet." I was too sick to be in shock. My daughter was never disrespectful to others. Part of me was so proud of her.

As I sat on the plane waiting for takeoff, I posted this post on my Facebook page, hit post and checked out mentally.

When the demon shows up, women, you love yourself. You run! If I could move my child and me out that next day I would! I could have died! Walking and trying to find the shuttle bus to hotel, I turned to the demon, and said, "I'm not feeling well." It said, "Come on; keep walking," not "What's wrong!" We arrived at the shuttle area, and I felt that I wanted to pass out.

I said, "I need water. I'm feeling delirious. Can you ask someone for water?"

The demon said, "I'm not asking anyone for water." Keep in mind I've never in my life been like this! Keep in mind also that I've been there for the demon! I was lying on the bench, keeled over, and my eyes felt like they were rolling back in my head. I could barely keep my eyes open.

I don't know when the bus came. I only heard someone yelling my name. I was not functioning, and I saw my daughter. I was floating toward her and got on the bus. They'd walked off and left me wobbling to the bus.

We got to the hotel, and I felt my daughter tap me. A concerned mom, I woke up. I don't remember how I made it into the lobby. I only remember I was lying on the blue chair. The demon yelled, "Yassin, I need your ID." My mouth felt like my tongue was ready to split in two. I yelled, "I need water!"

The demon said, "I'm not dealing with this," and walked away.

I screamed, "Someone, please get me some water!" All I remembered is a lady handing me a cup. I was in and out, non-responsive. I heard a lady say that she was a physician, and my pulse was weak. I drank water faster than they can bring it! I don't remember much. I was shivering; I was so cold! The EMTs were there, and I couldn't hear my daughter. I vaguely heard someone say that my pressure was one hundred ninety over I can't remember. Do I have pressure? I said. "No," I heard my daughter...I blanked out again.... someone asked where is the guy? I said, "He's an f'ing asshole!" Then someone said, "I can't believe he just left her!"

I heard them say I needed to go to the hospital. My pressure was way too high, and my heart rate was very fast. I said, no, my daughter. I don't know how long it took me to come to and be able to stand...Somehow, I made it to the room...

Demon didn't ask how I was feeling. 'Cause if he did, he would've known I was dizzy and my head was pounding.

The last words I told my daughter was that if any man did this to her—run!

The demon was depressed...right now I was in self-preservation....Mark Young help me get my child and me out of this. Getting on the plane! No weapon shall form against me!

The Lord is my Shepherd! Thank God for my daughter, who didn't leave her mother and stepped up to take over in my time of distress.

End of post...

I slept all the way through Sunday and all-day Monday. Periodically, I would get up and check my pressure. It went as high as one hundred ninety-five and as low as one hundred sixty-five. All my friends were worried about me. My sons' and my daughter's father, who lives in Kentucky, stayed on Facetime with her. All were very concerned.

My ex-husband was ready to get in the car and drive to Georgia. All he needed was for me to say the word.

My narcissist fiancé went to work that Monday. He came into the house after six, screaming on the phone to someone and as he walked up the stairs, he was telling them that we needed to leave his house, but he had signed an agreement.

My daughter and my sons heard him. I was still not well, and I was also weak. I was just walking out of the shower when he told the person he would call them back. He cornered me into the wall. As he moved closer to me, slowly, I took a step back until my behind hit the wall. I had no way to turn, and I felt threatened and defenseless. I looked down, and he was still wearing his gun. My guns were under my pillow in my office.

He demands that I give him money.

I was thinking money, *what money*? So, I asked him.

He replied, "The money for the hotel." Confused, I wasn't sure what hotel he was referring to, so I calmly asked how much it was. My goal was to have him move out of my way, so we would both be walking around armed, and I could protect my daughter.

He told me the amount was one hundred and some change.

The best weapon narcissists have against you is your fear. That's why I needed to be able to defend myself. No matter how terrified I might have felt, I knew I had to cut him off and show him I wasn't afraid. Show narcissists, you have the courage to fight for your life. Let them know that they have no power over you.

I remember reading this before on the cruise. He was standing at my office door as I was quietly writing the check. As I handed him the check, I pressed 911on my phone and grabbed my gun. I pointed it at him and said, "Don't even think about reaching for your gun. Before you reach for it, I'll empty every bullet into your body."

I made sure 911 recorded, indicating he was also armed.

He got scared and left the house. At that moment, I ran to my daughter's room and told her to start packing all of her items.

I called my ex-husband and told him to hack into his cameras and start recording.

My ex-husband was on video chat on my phone. My sons were on Facetime with their sister.

The police came and saw that we were safe. They advised me that since this was his house we should leave. I showed them that we were already packing.

I didn't feel safe going to any of the hotels in my area. The devil would find me. I wrote a Facebook post indicating that I'd called the police. Strangers I've never met were praying for us. One stranger who saw that I lived in North Georgia sent me a hotel reservation a little farther north, fully paid for two nights. I was so relieved that good people still existed in this cruel world.

It gave me the hope and strength to get my daughter to safety. The last thing I had the strength to do at that time was to call around looking for a place to stay.

God sent another angel.

He came back before we were all packed and as he walked in the door, I turned on Facebook live. The entire world was going to be my witness!

The narcissist remained calm and peaceful. He laid on his bed biting his fingernails like a two-year-old, turned on the television, and started watching a movie.

My daughter was shaken, and we calmly left, both dressed in our pajamas and bed slippers. I was confused, hurt, and just overwhelmed with all that had transpired.

At the hotel, my daughter said she wanted to go Facebook live to let everyone know we were okay. On camera, my daughter emotionally broke down, finally. She needed to. No seventeen-year-old should have to go through this. We cried ourselves to sleep, holding each other. For two days, we slept.

On the third day, I needed to step up and be a mom. We needed somewhere to live and fast.

I woke up to a message from a fella Diva inviting us to stay with her. I'd only met her on Facebook, and once when we finally greeted each other at a party.

I know I was not physically, mentally, or emotionally ready to look for housing just yet. I told her, yes. I was also working with my daughter's father to arrange for her to go to him. I knew she would be safe with him, and he knew how to get her better settled emotionally.

Once she was there, I could focus on my own needs.

Every product I owned, plus all my belongings, were at his house.

He texted me letting me know that he changed the locks, and I had to arrange a time with him to get them.

I was in total disbelief. He acted like he was the victim in danger, and I did this to him. I found an apartment less than ten blocks from his house. It was the only apartment complex that had immediate availability.

Numerous times, we agreed to meet. Each time, he canceled the meeting or didn't show up to open the door.

This frustrated me as I just wanted my belongings, so I could peacefully move on with my life. Finally, I had no other choice but to involve the police.

Two of my girlfriends from my hometown helped me to retrieve my items.

To my surprise, he threw all of my clothes on the garage floor. He stole all of the most expensive products I had purchased for my store. In front of my friends, he was being super nice. He thought they were falling for his charm. I knew they were just being cordial.

Boxes were everywhere in a two-bedroom apartment, but this was the beginning of a new chapter in my life. I was grateful and blessed to have friends who cared. They took the time to drive far and long to help.

It was now time for the healing to begin and for me to learn how to forgive his illness.

When the narcissist said, "I love you," he meant that he loved the way I made him feel when I worked hard to make him happy.

I sent him an email saying all the things I needed to say from day one. Then I blocked him.

He did find a way to respond by creating a new email address. I deleted it and never read it.

I've never seen him since that day. We still shop at the same stores, but I haven't run into him.

I stay in touch with his daughter and ex-wife. We have not spoken about what happened. In my gut, they know. Nothing needs to be explained.

Once my daughter was safe and sound with her father, I focused on my health. My pressure remained dangerously high.

One day, it rose to one hundred eighty-eight, and my diva friend, whom I was staying with, took me to the hospital and stayed with me. That was the first time a doctor asked me if I suffered from anxiety attacks. I had not.

I went to my primary physician who wanted to place me on high blood pressure medication, but I declined. In my gut, I knew this was not high blood pressure.

A few days later, my pressure was still high and fluctuating but not steady. I asked to see another doctor, a woman this time. Immediately, she told me it was anxiety. She told me that I was having silent anxiety attacks and asked if I had been exposed to trauma lately. I gave her the short version.

She placed me on anxiety medication. I was no stranger to mental health conditions. In the early stages, I was quite aware that with talk therapy I can regulate this silent killer—anxiety. I could not walk around like a ticking time bomb much longer.

It took at least two weeks before I had my ugly cry. When that excruciating and debilitating pain hits you so hard, you can't put off this feeling any longer. It's the pain we all try to avoid, distract ourselves and run away from. The reality was that it was officially over, and I was missing an important part of myself. The self-hate and doubt were having one big party in my mind. It makes you feel like you're completely lost, can't eat, work, or sleep. At that moment, you feel like this gut-wrenching pain is never going to end. This was just stage one shock, and I know there are more painful days like this ahead. I wondered if I was going to make it through as it felt like I just couldn't take any more emotionally.

I felt like I was going crazy!

After any breakup or loss, there's a lot going on in the brain and understanding how my body changes with heartbreak helped me realize that this is natural.

I knew the same flood of chemicals that caused me to be blissfully in love are the exact same chemicals that caused me to painfully suffer. I knew that my brain was in withdrawal.

It was due to that darn dopamine, the feel-good chemical that leaves you wanting more stimuli. My brain said, oh, wait, I'm not getting any more of this. What's going on here?

Although on a cognitive level I knew and accepted the relationship was over, the neurons in my brain were expecting its dose of dopamine.

Knowledge is power! Knowing the process, I called all of my friends, my support team. Every one of them adds comfort to every aspect of my life. In my phone calls to them, I said to look for the following:

1. Watch out for any strange or out-of-character posts on Facebook.

2. Do a spot check to see if I'm okay if I haven't posted by 10 p.m.

3. Text me no less than five times a day as I knew at least two of my closest friends would. Even though this drove me nuts, it was necessary.

4. Check on me to see if I ate and inquire about my health. I knew at least one of my family members would do so.

5. Check on me emotionally and physically, and I ended up having an entire Facebook squad of people I've never met do so.

I knew I couldn't do this alone. I also knew that this process was necessary for me to heal and grow. These were the three R's: react, reset, recharge and gain wisdom from the experience.

The next stage, denial, came the very next day. I could not believe how I returned to "Singleville."

It's important that you are aware of the stages in the event so that when the symptoms show up, you are ready to embrace it, as fighting only prolongs the healing process. I had no extra time to lose. I was losing revenue daily.

The third stage, anger, showed up a couple of days later. This breakup was costing me the loss of income. He had all my products. I had less than ten thousand dollars accessible to me. With this money, I had to pay first and last month's rent and security deposit for an apartment. In addition to housing here in the United States, I had a house in the Virgin Islands that needed repairs after getting hit by two category five hurricanes. Just like that, my bank account was quickly depleting, and my mind said this was all his fault!

For some reason, I skipped over stage four—depression. I'm thinking this happened since I knew that I was lucky to find out who he was before I married him. I knew I dodged a bullet and had nothing to be ashamed of. I did the right thing for my daughter and me.

Once I moved into the apartment, stage five—acceptance— hit me really hard. The last time I lived in an apartment was in the projects during my divorce. Knowing that less than a year ago I stayed in a four-bedroom house, I was beating myself up and couldn't stop. I wanted to believe that I didn't fall that hard this time. In my mind, it felt that way. I just couldn't shake that feeling of failure, even though I could see that I didn't fall but had just hit a snag in the road.

I know exactly when I need to reach and accept help. I picked up my phone and expressed to my therapist that it was time.

Therapy

Having a therapist who works for you is vital. I personally feel traditional therapy will not work for me because I've experienced too much in my life and have too many layers that I need to peel away. To cure me will require deep, intense, soulful, and holistic measures.

Just as you would be selective with a good bra, you should be just as selective with your mental health specialist.

Let the healing begin!

With each session, I had to feel pain, accept the reasons for my pain, forgive myself, cry and cleanse my mind.

The Goal

Silent Anxiety needed to go away for good. I also needed to get off the medication and rebuild my life for my daughter and long-term wellness for myself.

I longed to feel whole again.

The Root Cause

A good therapist will tune into finding the cause of your symptoms.

It takes as many sessions as needed to find it.

My first few sessions were finding forgiveness for his illness. Once I did this, true healing could start from within.

I felt the worst emotional session around my ninth or tenth session. That pain was worse than the breakup pain. That pain was playing on repeat in my subconscious mind for well over thirty-five years. For days after this session, I couldn't fully function, and all I wanted to do was sleep all day long—the brain's natural way of healing itself.

The Cause

There was a time in my life I thought, from prior treatments, that I was fully healed. I wrote a chapter in *Journey Untold* about it. I can stand in front of thousands of people and calmly paint a picture of the events.

The mind is one of the most intriguing organs in the body. That's why they are constantly doing research on how it works. The brain functions on its own, we only control less than ten percent daily.

Two events that I thought had no similarities whatsoever met at the same point of my emotions. Constantly, and unbeknownst to me, my brain connected the same feelings and essentially played those emotions over and over again.

The first emotion was abandonment that came from someone wanting to inflict harm on me. The second emotion was confusion.

Along with the day my mother ran behind me yelling, "Hold that child I'm going to kill her," my mind also registered the moment my ex-fiancé raised his hands and left me in the hotel lobby to die. Those two emotions negatively impacted my brain.

Treatment

Hypnosis was my way to heal and get back to the root cause of a distorted memory. Then, the painful negative memory must be replaced with a positive version of the incident.

Almost immediately after that session, my blood pressure started to reduce. With every session, other areas began to heal.

In less than a month, my pressure was fully stable and holding. My Silent Anxiety was now controlled.

I continued with my sessions, and my vision of my new life became super clear. My blessings from God, most I didn't pray for or expect, were pouring in.

In less than six months, my daughter and I purchased our new home in cash.

Therapy maybe an ongoing occurrence for me for the rest of my life. I've accepted this to be my truth, and I walk proudly in it.

I have a beautiful, magical, spiritual, amazing, grateful and joyful life. I'm living freely.

Chapter Ten: Am I too Strong?

I consider myself to be mentally strong. Let's face it, life has thrown me a dodgeball, bowling ball, wrecking ball, and sledgehammer in relationships. No matter what blunt force trauma I've endured, I've survived. With every hit, I've fallen in love with myself even more, unconditionally. Not many can say or even execute this process.

Over time, I've assessed myself and you might be able to relate.

Let me reintroduce to you my mental self.

I'm an incredible human being who has a mission of helping the world go around through my words and actions.

I possess incredible courage, and I'm fearless in pursuing my goals.

I take care of myself in an effort to preserve my mental wellness.

I empower others and offer hope along with gentle reminders that if you want something, go after it.

Even being fearless and through my outward thick-skinned appearance, toxicity, blindsided, can enter my life. These personality traits can and have at times made me the perfect patsy for people who use manipulation and love feeding their own egos.

One would think that a strong woman can easily identify manipulative skills, but, in fact, quite the opposite happens. We fall in love with that very impressionable skill set.

Let me explain. I'm an open book and straightforward. I'm not afraid to express to the world that I'm a woman with emotions.

With no hidden agenda, my insecurities are in the foreground. I'm unique and rightfully proud of this fact, so I embrace it.

While all these traits may not seem like a downfall, to a toxic person, my emotions can lead to their private playground. Why you may ask? As I fully expose myself, all of the guesswork is done.

Let the manipulation game begin.

Since I possess positive energy and an optimistic outlook toward life in general, my success is the reciprocal of that energy.

I'm also laidback and easygoing, but I am always in the pursuit of infinite joy. My qualities are my amazing gift. Does this sound like you as well?

There are those who love being around me because I have a huge heart and owing to my life's experiences, I can be sincere and very giving of my emotions. I believe that happiness and joy should be passed on. I'm constantly thinking of ways to help others.

However, toxic people are fueled and intrigued by these characteristics. It's new and different to them. They want to try it, but not own that energy within themselves. They just want to test drive it, per say.

The ultimate goal of these manipulators is to unravel my weakness in an attempt to use it against me. That's their weapon of choice.

It takes me a long time to get upset or to reach my enough stage, and that is also my weakness. Toxic people test my threshold, but once I react, they know at that moment they "Own my Power" without me even realizing I gave it to them. It's like a sniper on the hill who stayed still for days and months learning by watching everything you do. With their knowledge and observations, they silently create an imbalance of power shift.

While they are learning about me, in my mind, it looks like love. Can you relate?

Time and time again, a toxic person will present themselves as the "victim," and my caring, kind nature forgives and finds compassion, forgetting that I'm the victim here!

Now, here's the question: How do I stop letting toxic individuals into my life, period? Keep a mental note and understand that toxic people are trying to convince you to give up your power to serve themselves. Take a step back and recognize that. You may even make a journal of the times that an individual has made you feel violated.

Know your rights, believe in your rights and *own* your rights.

You have the right to the following:

1.) Say no, without guilt!
2.) Express your feelings and emotions without ridicule or judgments.
3.) Set your own priorities.
4.) Have different opinions.
5.) Be happy.
6.) Walk away proudly.
7.) Know that it is *not* your job to change them.

8.) Most importantly, to take care of and protect yourself from being threatened or harmed physically, mentally or emotionally.

Constantly ask yourself, "Do I feel good about myself when I'm around them or when I am away from them?" If the answer is no, it's okay to crank your power button up for your own self-preservation.

Once you *own* your rights, you become vigilant toward other's behavior. Your tolerance level will begin to tell that voice in your head "oh, no, this is not for me," and your woman's intuition will trigger your "exit stage left strategy."

Your level of discernment will beam and glow.

In the moments of uncertainty, ask the following questions to a toxic person and watch their behavior shift to confusion. What you're ultimately doing is putting up a mirror in front of them, so they are forced to see their own reflection.

1.) Does what you are expecting of me seem reasonable to you?
2.) Are you asking or telling me?
3.) Please tell me the benefits I'm getting out of this.

As you can imagine, these questions will throw a curveball at that moment. They may pause, as that's the result of your in their face self-reflection, but you show them that you are very aware of their intent.

While this strategy works on most, please be aware that if the person is living with a mental health disorder, it's very possible that this may show zero effects in their behavior. Mental health disorders tend to have an invisible cape beyond the naked eye. In this case, you will have to revert to asking if you're happy in their presence.

From there, you will know exactly what to do or not do. Ultimately, it's your power to reclaim and maintain. Those that infuriate, anger or upsets me, makes me feel sad, lonely, mad and make me show a side of me I'm not proud of controls me. I will not allow them to take my power. Today and *always, I'll own my power.*

I would love for you to write these words down. Stick them on your mirrors, your car's dashboard, on your desk at work, or even by your phone charger. Read them many times throughout the day so that subconsciously, your mindset *will* manifest change.

To those who believe "I am too Strong," I say this. Fully exposing myself as a strong woman, my weakness is that I crave real connection. Acceptance of this weakness gives me my power at all times. Just like that, I no longer have a weakness!

I get attached to things that I've never felt before because I'm vulnerable, loving, and strong.

I have hope in human beings. Despite my battles with love, I firmly believe in true love.

I get that I'm intimidating. I understand you're afraid and anxious. You may not have met someone like me before, so your willingness to please me confuses you.

My message to you is don't be scared to love me and be grateful for the once in a lifetime experience.

Watching myself standing in such a joyful place spiritually, mentally, emotionally, physically, and financially warms my heart daily. I've come a long way on this journey even when I lost myself and my hope. I'm blessed to have never lost faith while gaining the power of self-love. I honestly didn't think that could be possible. I rebound from being internally broken to blissfully in love within. This is how I've moved Beyond the Love Curse.

There is no fear in love, only faith. My heart lights me up daily. God has shown his favor to me. I trust in him

I have always been a goal-oriented person with a well-thought-out plan, and I've experienced a lot of personal and professional success (despite my fair share of setbacks) simply because I knew where I wanted to go and how I was going to get there.

I'm always designing my life. I write down my own rules for happiness. Walking into my purpose felt overwhelming, but in hindsight, it was worth the soul searching. I have found true fulfillment and joy in everything I'm doing.

How did I walk into my purpose is one of the most popular questions I'm asked?

I started by identifying the things that truly excite me, things I'm naturally drawn to, and things I'm compelled to do and then I gave my energy to accomplish the goals.

Pushing yourself requires energy, and eventually that energy must be restored. But when you are being pulled in a direction, no energy is required.

The more I explored my strengths and passions, the more I realized how they are connected to my experiences and my journey. Ultimately, my purpose appeared right in front of me.

Ask yourself:

1.) How will this shifting of my mindset change my identity?

2.) Who do I want to become?

3.) Reflect on yourself and your purpose daily.

You are the biggest most important project in your life— not your relationship, not your career, not your children. You!

I became more successful in my life when I truly aligned myself with my purpose. Every day that I got closer to understanding my why and fulfilling my purpose, I became a happier person.

Life can leave so many of us reeling, asking "Why me?" or "How did I get here?" Writing and expressing my thoughts publicly exposed me to freedom of the mind, body, and soul. It's fun and cathartic for me. In utilizing my struggles, showing I'm human, and combining my passions, I've found joy in walking in my truth.

You now have the steps to put your own beautiful happy life blueprint together. You owe it to yourself; trust me, the rewards will be more than you can imagine.

Through persistence, self-knowledge, prayer, commitment, optimism, a resolute trust in God and the building of your own personal moral strength, you can enjoy the blessings of a deeper faith and face the difficulties of life with courage and confidence. - Norman Vincent Peale

I recently returned from a twelve-day, self-actualization vacation to Asia. I visited Bali, Korea, Singapore and two cities in Thailand. While on this vacation, I pushed myself to accomplish so many fears such as:

Flying on a plane out of the United States by myself,

Surviving turbulence flying into monsoon rainstorms four times,

Traveling with others whom I had not met in person,

Experience adventures that were terrifying such as petting a live tiger, swinging off a cliff,

Climbing mountains to visit holy temples,

Trusting others with my truth and my disorders and knowing that I would be ok,

I have a newfound appreciation for the life I have, this trip confirmed that I am exactly where God intended me to be. I found serenity and soulful love inside myself.

I sat between the gates of Heaven

Bali Indonesia

The below quote expresses my takeaway lesson learned from my adventures.

We spend more, but have less; we buy more, but enjoy it less. We have smaller families; more conveniences, but less time. We have more degrees but less sense; more knowledge, but less judgement; more experts, yet more problems; more medicine, but less wellness. We spend too recklessly, laugh too little, drive too fast, get angry too quickly, stay up too late, get up too tired, read too little, watch TV too much and pray too seldom. We have multiplied our possessions but reduced our values. We talk too much, love too seldom and hate too often. We've learned how to make a living, but not a life. We've added years to life, not life to years.

~ Bob Moorehead

I am enjoying understanding how to love myself more, a huge steppingstone towards me accepting that reciprocated love. I'm ready and here for it!

Through deep soul searching, I'm still in therapy learning how to break down guarded walls, building trusting healthy relationships and discovering how to embrace various types of love from the others; the love God will bring forth to love Yassin Hall.

A message to my future friends, acquittances, and lover,

Give me you in bits and pieces that will nature my heart. Love me in thousands of ways different from the love you have offered others, for I'm uniquely healing.

Take me to places soulfully that I will never be able to walk to.

Make me feel every inch of your thoughts. In turn, I will open my mind, soul and my body.

Run your fingers through my soul to understand how I'm feeling without my having to say a word.

Enjoy purposely cleansing my gorgeous life experiences with me. See the poetry in my pain turned passion and embrace it with empathy. Create poetic harmony to maintain faith together.

Listen to the music I'm playing in my mind when I'm silent as the tunes will confess my deep inner thoughts to you.

Come forth with the knowledge and understanding that loving me cannot be measured. I'm a deep thinker; I know.

The lyrics from Monica's song "Commitment" is a perfect reflection of my words above.

It don't take much, a little affection,
'Cause some of your time, that's all that I'm asking for,
Feels like this dream will ever come true,
I just want somebody who knows how to listen,
And give me attention, who won't break my heart,
I have good intentions,
I ain't hard to please; I don't need a lot, Just show me that
you care
Can you be there when I need you most?
And when I say I don't, make me feel secure forever,
I just need someone to love me when it's hard to,
I can trust with all my issues,
Someone who is patient and consistent,
I need good sex and commitment,
From somebody loyal, understanding, who won't change
up,
Take advantage of my emotions or my feelings,
I don't want money,
I rather have somebody real,
I can be myself in front who makes me mad and make me
cry,
Who knows what it means to sacrifice,

If I'm havin' a bad day, you know just what to say,

I can show you all my thoughts and where my demon's
play,

And you won't use them against me, You rather use them to
leave me.

Can't you be there when I need you most?

Make me feel beautiful, give free assurance, forever.

- Monica

To my future husband, I'm looking forward to meeting you.
I'll enjoy watching you fall asleep and miss you until
you're awake.

To my future friends and acquaintances, we will celebrate
life, our successes together and will positively endure
whatever God puts in our path and rise together.

Until we meet again..."The Journey Unfolds" joyfully ever
after...Yassin

PERSONAL THERAPISTS RECOMMENDATIONS

For myself, I prefer in home therapy. I am comfortable staying in my house (my safe space). Wither it's by Skype, Zoom or in person. This method works well for my family and me.

Jacqui Letran is a Mindset Mentor who dedicates her life's work to help her clients stop their critical inner voice, build confidence and self-trust and embrace a resilient mindset needed to create a happy, successful life.

(714) 654-3211

Types of services - Healing Mind Hypnotherapy
http://healingmindshypnotherapy.com/

Adapt Behavioral Services www.adapt-fl.com

Orlando, Maitland, Ormond Beach & Kissimmee, FL

(407) 622-0444

Focus on identifying life patterns, triggers and other factors that create or contribute to your symptoms. Teach you the skills to use to overcome or manage them.

NAMI.ORG – FREE Mental Health Support

NAMI Basics is a class for parents, guardians and other family caregivers who provide care for youth (age 22 or younger) who are experiencing mental health symptoms.

NAMI Family-to-Family is a class for families, significant others and friends of people with mental health conditions. The course is designed to facilitate a better understanding of mental health conditions, increase coping skills and empower participants to become advocates for their family members.

NAMI Homefront is a class for families, caregivers and friends of military service members and veterans with mental health conditions.

NAMI Peer-to-Peer is a class for adults with mental health conditions. The course is designed to encourage growth, healing and recovery among participants.

NAMI Family & Friends is a 4-hour seminar that informs and supports people who have loved ones with a mental health condition. Participants learn about diagnoses, treatment, recovery, communication strategies, crisis preparation and NAMI resources.

NAMI Connection is a support group for people with mental health conditions. Groups meet weekly, every other week or monthly, depending on location.

NAMI Family Support Group is a support group for family members, significant others and friends of people with mental health conditions.

NAMI Smarts for Advocacy is a hands-on advocacy training program that helps people living with mental illness, friends and family transform their passion and lived experience into skillful grassroots advocacy.

United States & U.S Territories Therapists Directory
Not personal recommendations but they fall in line with the TYPES of Therapy I believe in.

Name	Telephone	Website	Type of Therapy
AL			
Alabama Hypnosis Clinic	(205) 322-7284	www.pathfoundation.com/	Hypnotherapy
New Perspectives Counseling & Consulting, LLC	(205) 960-9150	newperspectivesconsult.com/	Humanistic
Rainwater Counseling Madison	(256) 272-4223	www.rainwatercounseling.com/services/	Cognitive Behavioral Therapy
Rehabilitation Counseling, LLC	(205) 598-2447 ext. 103	www.rehabilitation-counseling.com/	Integrative or Holistic Therapy
Rocket City Counselor	(256) 665-9966	rocketcitycounselor.com/	Trauma-Focused Cognitive Behavioral Therapy (TF-CBT)

AK

Mindful Exchanges	(907) 745-7799	www.mindfulexchanges.com/	Hypnotherapy
Refocus Counseling	(907) 521-8504	refocuscounseling.com/	Humanistic
Mental & Behavioral Healthcare Services, LLC	(855) 463-9581	www.nfearringtontherapy.com/	Cognitive Behavioral Therapy
Recovery Waters Counseling	(907) 406-7640	www.recoverywaterscounseling.com/	Integrative or Holistic Therapy
Wisdom Traditions Counseling & Wellness	(907) 770-3656	awisdomcenter.com/	Trauma-Focused Cognitive Behavioral Therapy (TF-CBT)

AZ

Tucson Counseling	(520) 873-8562	tucsoncounseling.org/index.html	Hypnotherapy
Lifeline Professional Counseling	(480) 725-2796	lifelinepcs.com/#home	Humanistic
De Novo	(520) 395-2369	www.denovowellnesscenter.com/	Cognitive Behavioral Therapy
Arcadia Counseling Center	(602) 218-6901	arcadiacounselingcenter.com/	Integrative or Holistic Therapy
Purple Heart Behavioral Health, LLC	(602) 529-8120	purpleheartbh.com/	Trauma-Focused Cognitive Behavioral

AR

	Scheider Therapy Services	(501) 438-0118	www.scheidertherapyservices.com/	Hypnotherapy
	Le Counseling Services	(479) 888-4679	www.lecounselingservices.com/	Humanistic
	Create Healing Counseling Services PLLC	(501) 940-6135	createcounseling.com/	Cognitive Behavioral Therapy
	Journey Counseling, PLLC	(479) 657-6636	Journey Counseling, PLLC	Integrative or Holistic Therapy
CA	Avidus Therapy, LLC	(501) 615-7044	www.avidustherapy.com/	Trauma-Focused Cognitive Behavioral Therapy (TF-CBT)
	Farooq Malik Therapy	(415) 964-3281	www.farooqm.com/	Hypnotherapy
	Peace n Balance	(424) 264-9058	www.peacenbalance.net/	Humanistic
	Sharon Yu Therapy	(626) 538-7561	www.sharonyutherapy.com/	Cognitive Behavioral Therapy
	Finding Love for Today	(951) 343-7193	www.findinglove4today.com/	Integrative or Holistic Therapy
	Andrew Susskind	(310) 281-8681	westsidetherapist.com/index.html	Trauma-Focused
CO				
	SonderMind			

241

	: Mr. Kyle Brown			
	Heart Centered Counseling	(970) 310-3406	heartcenteredcounselors.com/	Humanistic
	Your Family Matters, LLC	(719) 310-9235	www.yfmllc.com/	Cognitive Behavioral Therapy
	Valerie Varan	(303) 547-8327	www.heartlivingspirit.com/	Integrative or Holistic Therapy
	Alpine Lakes Counseling Center	(303) 219-9548	alpinelakescounselingcenter.com/	Trauma-Focused Cognitive Behavioral Therapy (TF-CBT)
CT	Dr. Inessa Zaleski	(800) 929-2256	calmness.com/go/	Hypnotherapy
	Courage Counseling, LLC	(860) 785-6222	www.couragecc.com/	Humanistic
	It Is Time, LLC	(475) 289-2500	itistimellc.com/home.php	Cognitive Behavioral Therapy
	Elyon Professional Counseling LLC	(203) 570-1568	www.elyonprofessionalcounseling.com/	Integrative or Holistic Therapy
	Overcoming Life's Obstacles Counseling	(203) 805-9919	www.olo-counseling.com/	Trauma-Focused Cognitive Behavioral
DE	First State Hypnosis	(302) 547-4645	www.firststatehypnosis.com/	Hypnotherapy

	Journey Two Serenity	(302) 416-6805	journeytwoserenity.net/	Humanistic
	Delaware Family Center	(302) 995-9600	delawarefamilycenter.com/	Cognitive Behavioral Therapy
	Partners in Health and Wellbeing (PHW)	(302) 655-2627	partnersinhealthandwellbeing.com /home/	Integrative or Holistic Therapy
	Allie F. Miller, M.A., L.M.F.T.	(302) 287-3443	www.amillerlmft.com/	Trauma-Focused Cognitive Behavioral Therapy (TF-CBT)
FL	Clinical Hypnothera py & NLP Life Coaching	(561) 266-3669	www.getjoyful.com/	Hypnotherapy
	Compassion ate Healing, LLC	(954) 654-7377	www.compassionatehealingflorida .com/	Humanistic
	Capital City Counseling Services	(850) 329-0102	capitalcitycounselingservices.com	Cognitive Behavioral Therapy
	Fun-Filled Love	(352) 215-5165	www.funfilledlove.com/	Integrative or Holistic Therapy
	Spectrum Recovery Solutions	(239) 595-3022	spectrumrecoverysolutions.com	Trauma-Focused Cognitive Behavioral
GA	Pure			

243

Hypnosis				
Completely Psyched, LLC	(404) 585-7375	www.completelypsyched.com/	Humanistic
Thriveworks Counseling and Coaching	(678) 853-5849	thriveworks.com/mcdonough-counseling/	Cognitive Behavioral Therapy
Gretchen Torbert, Ph.D., CHLC	(800) 401-3603	www.teachersacrosstheworld.com/	Integrative or Holistic Therapy
Smileology Counseling Services, LLC	(404) 800-1218	www.smileologycounseling.com	Trauma-Focused Cognitive Behavioral Therapy (TF-CBT)
HI				
	Hawaii Hypnosis Center	(808) 221-7353	www.hawaiihypnosiscenter.com/	Hypnotherapy
	Emily R. Hew, LMFT	(808) 495-0210	www.emilyhewcounseling.com/	Humanistic
	Leap of Faith Counseling, LLC	(808) 400-9845	www.leapoffaithcounseling.com/	Cognitive Behavioral Therapy
	Desiree C. Cabint	(808) 284-1807	www.drcabinte.com/	Integrative or Holistic Therapy
	The Counseling Center Hawaii	(808) 527-4470	www.counselingcenterhawaii.com/	Trauma-Focused Cognitive Behavioral
	Something Different		www.somethingdifferentcounselin	

Counseling			
Freedom In Choices LLC	(208) 595-2490	www.freedominchoices.com/	Humanistic
Seeking Serenity Therapy LLC	(208) 505-8813	www.seekingserenitytherapy.com/	Cognitive Behavioral Therapy
The Bridge Counseling	(208) 410-4866	www.bridgecounselingllc.com/	Integrative or Holistic Therapy
The Art of Recovery, Mary Beth Puri	(208) 250-2724	www.theartofedrecovery.com/	Trauma-Focused Cognitive Behavioral Therapy (TF-CBT)

IL

Meridian Peak Hypnosis	(630) 686-2626	www.meridianpeakhypnosis.com/	Hypnotherapy
Stenzel Clinical	(630) 588-1201	stenzelclinical.com/	Humanistic
The OCD and Anxiety center	(331) 256-1823	www.theocdandanxietycenter.com/	Cognitive Behavioral Therapy
Within Holistic Counseling	(773) 226-5603	www.chicagoholisticcounseling.com/	Integrative or Holistic Therapy
House Calls Counseling	(847) 256-2000	www.housecallscounseling.com/	Trauma-Focused Cognitive Behavioral Therapy (TF-CBT)

IN

Indiana Integrative Hypnosis	(317) 706-0306	www.indianaintegrativehypnosis.com/	Hypnotherapy
Three Stones Counseling	(317) 661-2986	www.threestonescounseling.com/	Humanistic
Way Point Counseling	(812) 359-0150	waypointcounselingin.com/	Cognitive Behavioral Therapy
Be Your Very Best	(219) 663-3900	www.dianagovert.com/	Integrative or Holistic Therapy
Encouraging Insight Counseling Services, LLC.	(317) 755-7442	www.encouraginginsight.com/trauma	Trauma-Focused Cognitive Behavioral Therapy (TF-CBT)

IA

Hypnotic Solutions	(563) 581-9224	helpthroughhypnosis.com/	Hypnotherapy
Liberty Therapy Associates, LLC	(319) 774-3759	www.libertytherapyassociates.com/	Humanistic
Center For Healing And Hope, LLC	(712) 256-9660	www.healingandhopellc.com/	Cognitive Behavioral Therapy
Melissa Maranda Holistic Counseling	(563) 570-2533	www.counselingwithmelissa.com/	Integrative or Holistic Therapy
B.P.R. Therapy, Mediation & Coaching			Trauma-Focused Cognitive Behavioral Therapy

				(TF-CBT)
KS				
	New Day Hypnotherapy	(913) 908-6907	newdayhypno.com/	Hypnotherapy
	True Self Counseling	(913) 991-3974	trueselfcounseling.com/	Humanistic
	Wichita Counseling and Coaching Center LLC	(316) 729-9965	www.wichita-counseling.com/	Cognitive Behavioral Therapy
	Sana Holistic Care	(816) 304-0434	sanakc.com/	Integrative or Holistic Therapy
	Wild Hope Kansas City	(816) 944-3687	wildhopekansascity.com/	Trauma-Focused Cognitive Behavioral Therapy (TF-CBT)
KY				
	KY Hypnosis	(859) 553-4616	www.kyhypnosis.com/	Hypnotherapy
	Northstar Counseling Center	(502) 414-1301	northstarcounselingcenter.com/	Humanistic
	Louisville Counseling Associates, LLC	(502) 883-6613	louisvillecounseling.weebly.com/	Cognitive Behavioral Therapy
	Bridge Counseling and Wellness	(502) 694-9488	bridgemindbody.com/	Integrative or Holistic Therapy
				Trauma-Focused Cognitive

			Behavioral Therapy (TF-CBT)

LA

Life Transformations LLC	(318) 868-6197	hypnosisovereasy.com/	Hypnotherapy
New Orleans Multicultural Institute of Counseling	(504) 814-4480	www.nomicllc.com/	Humanistic
Behavioral Health Counseling and Consulting	(504) 556-2635	behavioralhealthcnc.com/	Cognitive Behavioral Therapy
Holistic Life Approach	(985) 276-8119	www.holisticlifeapproach.com/	Integrative or Holistic Therapy
Ligia Soileau, LCSW-BACS	(225) 442-9034	www.brtherapy.com/	Trauma-Focused Cognitive Behavioral Therapy (TF-CBT)

ME

Atlantic Hypnotherapy	(207) 807-6270	www.portlandmainehypnosis.com/	Hypnotherapy
Cornerstones of Maine	(800) 588-6898	www.cornerstonesofmaine.com/	Humanistic
Susan Penza-Clyve, PhD	(207) 756-4278	www.portlandcbt.com/	Cognitive Behavioral Therapy
Maine Holistic Counseling	(207) 620-4691	mainehealthmhc.wixsite.com/holistic	Integrative or Holistic Therapy

MD	Redefining Therapy LLC	(207) 994-8915	keitaawhitten.com/	Trauma-Focused Cognitive Behavioral Therapy (TF-CBT)
	Attention to Living	(410) 382-0518	www.attentiontoliving.com/	Hypnotherapy
	Pathways 4 Mental Health	(443) 877-6959	www.pathways4mentalhealth.org/	Humanistic
	Solomon Counseling	(410) 417-7576	www.solomoncounseling.com/	Cognitive Behavioral Therapy
	Sun Point Wellness	(301) 541-8072	www.sunpointwellness.com/silver spring	Integrative or Holistic Therapy
MA	Anchored Hope Therapy	(443) 291-8090	anchoredhopetherapy.com/about-us/	Trauma-Focused Cognitive Behavioral Therapy (TF-CBT)
	Integral Hypnosis - Boston	(617) 964-4800	www.integralhypnosis.com/	Hypnotherapy
	North Suburban Counseling	(781) 246-3388	www.northsuburbancounseling.net/	Humanistic
	Life Changes Group	(617) 354-4450	lifechangesgroup.com/wp/	Cognitive Behavioral Therapy
	Center for Integrative Counseling			Integrative

	and Wellness			
	The Wholeness Center	(508) 580-3800	www.thewholenesscenterma.org/	Trauma-Focused Cognitive Behavioral Therapy (TF-CBT)
MI	Focused Solutions Hypnothera py by Kim Manning	(248) 433-3075	www.focusedsolutions.com/	Hypnotherapy
	Humanistic Wellness Center	(734) 639-2262	humanisticwellnesscenter.com/	Humanistic
	Tiffany Turner, LMSW	(734) 433-5100	www.thrivingmindsbehavioralheal th.com/	Cognitive Behavioral Therapy
	Rooted Counseling	(724) 454-9024	rootedcounselingmi.com/	Integrative or Holistic Therapy
MN	The Traini Counseling Group	(810) 877-6343	openpathcollective.org/clinicians/y asmin-al-traini/	Trauma-Focused Cognitive Behavioral Therapy (TF-CBT)
	The FARE Hypnosis Center	(952) 934-1315	farehypnosis.com/	Hypnotherapy
	Relate Counseling Center	(952) 932-7277	www.relatemn.org/	Humanistic
	Conscious			Cognitive

	Healing Counseling	com/	Behavioral Therapy
	Integrated Life Counseling Center	(612) 379-6363	integratedlifecounseling.com/	Integrative or Holistic Therapy
MS	Family Revelations	(651) 319-6484	northlandcounseling.org/mental-health/tf-cbt/	Trauma-Focused Cognitive Behavioral Therapy (TF-CBT)
	My Relaxation Therapy	(601) 737-5806	www.myrelaxationtherapy.com/	Hypnotherapy
	Hope Enrichment Center	(662) 536-6210	www.hopeenrichmentcenter.com/	Humanistic
	Lotus Place Counseling	(601) 427-5158	lotusplacecounseling.com/about/	Cognitive Behavioral Therapy
	Shanti Yoga & Counseling	(228) 284-2337	www.shantiyogaandcounseling.com/	Integrative or Holistic Therapy
	Encounter Community Counseling Center	(601) 613-1240	www.etriplec.com/	Trauma-Focused Cognitive Behavioral Therapy (TF-CBT)

MO			
	Joan Krueger Hypnosis	(314) 962-7558	www.jfkhypnosis.com/	Hypnotherapy

	Diversified Health and Wellness Center	(844) GO2-DHWC (462-3492)	www.diversifiedhwc.com/mental-health-counseling	Humanistic
	Heartland Counseling Center	(573) 218-9699	www.heartlandcounselingcenter.com/	Cognitive Behavioral Therapy
	Drops Of Hope Integrative Care Center	(636) 578-2836	www.amaranthcounseling.com/	Integrative or Holistic Therapy
MT	Family Forward	(314) 968-2350	familyforwardmo.org/	Trauma-Focused Cognitive Behavioral Therapy (TF-CBT)
	Inner Wisdom Hypnotherapy	(406) 544-2486	www.innerwisdommissoula.com/	Hypnotherapy
	Voices Counseling	(406) 412-6556	voicescounseling.com/	Humanistic
	Inner Quest Counseling	(406) 539-5569	www.inner-questcounseling.com/	Cognitive Behavioral Therapy
	Imagine Health	(406) 892-4406	www.imaginehealth.net/	Integrative or Holistic Therapy
NE	Riverside Therapy, LLC	(406) 698-5299	www.riversidetherapyllc.com/	Trauma-Focused Cognitive
	Nebraska Counseling & Hypnosis			

	Center			
	Focus C3 PC	(531) 233-0912	www.focusc3.com/index.html	Humanistic
	Affinity Community Counseling	(531) 233-0909	www.affinitycommunitycounseling.com/	Cognitive Behavioral Therapy
	Wholeness Healing Center	(308) 382-5297	wholenesshealing.com/	Integrative or Holistic Therapy
	Omaha Trauma Therapy	(531) 444-1963	www.omahatraumatherapy.com/	Trauma-Focused Cognitive Behavioral Therapy (TF-CBT)
NV	Be Limitless Hypnosis	(702) 475-0764	www.belimitlesshypnosisacademy.com/	Hypnotherapy
	Person-Holistic Innovations	(702) 518-4532	personholisticinnovations.com/services/	Humanistic
	Next Chapter Therapy	(702) 508-5920	nextchaptertherapy.com/	Cognitive Behavioral Therapy
	Kayenta Therapy	(702) 438-7800	kayentatherapy.com/	Integrative or Holistic Therapy
	Healthy Minds	(702) 622-2491	www.healthymindslv.com/	Trauma-Focused Cognitive Behavioral Therapy (TF-CBT)
NH	A New You Center For Hypnosis	(603) 749-6463	anewyoucenter.com/	Hypnotherapy
	Grow Your			

	Name	Phone	Website	Therapy
	Own Way Counseling Services, LLC			
	Mill House Counseling	(603) 742-1373	www.millhousecounseling.com/	Cognitive Behavioral Therapy
	Blackbird's Daughter Botanicals	(802) 578-7931	www.blackbirdsdaughter.com/about	Integrative or Holistic Therapy
NJ	Alliance Counseling Services	(603) 952-4630	alliancecounselingservices.net/	Trauma-Focused Cognitive Behavioral Therapy (TF-CBT)
	Metro Hypnosis Center LLC	(201) 477-0265	www.metrohypnosiscenter.com/	Hypnotherapy
	Dr. Mark Lyall	(973) 798-2536	www.drmarklyall.com/	Humanistic
	Strength For Change	(973) 770-7600	strengthforchange.com/	Cognitive Behavioral Therapy
	Holistic Counseling Services	(856) 318-1581	aholisticlife.org/	Integrative or Holistic Therapy
	Portrait Health Centers	(732) 702-3784	www.portraithealthcenters.com/	Trauma-Focused Cognitive Behavioral
NM	Reclaim Wellness	(575) 523-8951	www.reclaimlc.com/	Hypnotherapy
	Gregory Weeks Counseling	(575) 219-6260	www.gregoryweekscounseling.com/	Humanistic

254

	Mindful Counseling LLC	(505) 899-9329	www.mindfulcounseling.org/	Cognitive Behavioral Therapy
	Rising Sun Holistic Counseling	(575) 571-9980	www.risingsuncounseling.com/	Integrative or Holistic Therapy
NY	Daniel Mintie, LCSW	(575) 758-2795	danielmintie.com/	Trauma-Focused Cognitive Behavioral Therapy (TF-CBT)
	Advanced Hypnosis Center NY	(212) 585-4430	hypnosis.ahcenter.com/	Hypnotherapy
	New York Person-Centered Resource Center	(212) 989-6086	www.nypcrc.org/	Humanistic
	Soho Cognitive	(212) 925-9833	www.sohocognitive.com/	Cognitive Behavioral Therapy
	Heart And Soul Transformational Therapy	(917) 231-0202	heartandsoultherapy.com/	Integrative or Holistic Therapy
	The Feeling Good Center of New York	(914) 315-7950	www.feelinggoodcenter.com/	Trauma-Focused Cognitive Behavioral Therapy (TF-CBT)
NC				

	Carolina Family Hypnosis	(919) 453-2519	www.carolinafamilyhypnosis.com/	Hypnotherapy
	Woodfin Wellness	(828) 252-1086	www.woodfinwellness.com/	Humanistic
	Live N Joy Counseling Services, PC	(704) 754-4726	www.livenjoycounseling.org/	Cognitive Behavioral Therapy
	Center For Holistic Healing	(336) 841-4307	www.chhtree.com/	Integrative or Holistic Therapy
ND	Springboard Therapy	(919) 638-3946	springboardtherapync.com/	Trauma-Focused Cognitive Behavioral Therapy (TF-CBT)
	Hypnosis Connection	(239) 322-4586	hypnosisconnection.com/	Hypnotherapy
	Insight Counseling	(701) 401-0886	www.insightcounselingnd.com/	Humanistic
	Solid Ground	(701) 490-8092	solidgroundvc.com/	Cognitive Behavioral Therapy
	Inner Reflection Holistic Health Center	(701) 340-4514	innerreflection.abmp.com/	Integrative or Holistic Therapy
OH	Nu Vation Health Services	(701) 401-5203 x16	www.nuvationhealthservices.com/	Trauma-Focused Cognitive
	Family Hypnosis Centers of			

Ohio			
Humanistic Counseling Center, LLC	(216) 839-2273	www.humanisticcounselingcenter.com/	Humanistic
Cindy Jesse ONLINE Life Coaching and Therapy	(513) 706-5950	www.cindyjesse.com/	Cognitive Behavioral Therapy
Bridging The Gap Holistic Services, LLC	(513) 549-0854	www.btgholisticservices.com/	Integrative or Holistic Therapy
Positive Solutions Counseling Center	(937) 719-0255	www.positivesolutionscounselingcenter.com/	Trauma-Focused Cognitive Behavioral Therapy (TF-CBT)

OK			
Tammy Coin And The Doors of Wellness	(405) 410-1507	thedoorsofwellness.com/index.html	Hypnotherapy
Instilling Hope & Wellness LLC	(405) 374-4998	instillinghopellc.com/about-us/	Humanistic
Abundant Life Family Therapy	(405) 313-8452	www.abundantlifefamilytherapy.com/	Cognitive Behavioral Therapy
New Vision Counseling and Consulting	(405) 921-7776	www.newvisioncounseling.org/	Integrative or Holistic Therapy
Focis			Trauma-Focused Cognitive Behavioral

257

				Therapy (TF-CBT)
OR				
	Intuitive Hypnosis	(503) 312-4660	www.intuitivehypnosisportland.com/	Hypnotherapy
	Irma E. Llanes, MA, LPC	(503) 332-3394	www.irmallanes.com/	Humanistic
	A Work in Progress	(971) 229-1797	a-workinprogress.com/	Cognitive Behavioral Therapy
	Alive Holistic Counseling	(541) 357-3248	www.aliveholisticcounseling.com/	Integrative or Holistic Therapy
	Options Counseling and Family Services	(503) 352-3260	wp.options.org/locations/beaverton/	Trauma-Focused Cognitive Behavioral Therapy (TF-CBT)
PA				
	PA Hypnosis Center	(724) 934-8446	www.pahypnosiscenter.com/	Hypnotherapy
	Humanistic Therapy Center	(610) 910-8500	www.humanistictherapycenter.com/	Humanistic
	Seth J. Gillihan, Ph.D., LLC	(610) 649-3265	sethgillihan.com/	Cognitive Behavioral Therapy
	Serenity Wellness Center	(610) 565-6627	www.serenitywellnessllc.com/	Integrative or Holistic Therapy
	Philadelphia Center For Emotionally Focused		www.philadelphiacenterforeft.org	Trauma-Focused Cognitive Behavioral Therapy

				(TF-CBT)
RI	Providence Hypnosis Center	(401) 351-1700	providencehypnosiscenter.com/	Hypnotherapy
	Inner You Counseling Center	(401) 773-7116	inneryoucounselingri.com/	Humanistic
	Anchor Counseling Center	(401) 475-9979	www.anchorcounselingcenter.com/	Cognitive Behavioral Therapy
	The Holistic Heart	(401) 441-8449	www.holisticheartri.com/	Integrative or Holistic Therapy
	The Wellness Center	(401) 461-9355	www.thewellnesscenterri.com/	Trauma-Focused Cognitive Behavioral Therapy (TF-CBT)
SC	TrueHypnosis, LLC	(843) 252-0573	truehypnosis.com/	Hypnotherapy
	Charleston Counseling Center	(843) 501-1099	www.charlestoncounseling.org/	Humanistic
	South Carolina Counseling & Consulting Services, LLC	(803) 335-1199	www.sccacs.com/	Cognitive Behavioral Therapy
	The Healing Arts Center	(843) 631-6422	www.healingartscentersc.com/	Integrative or Holistic Therapy
				Trauma-Focused

LLC			Cognitive Behavioral Therapy (TF-CBT)
SD			
Heal With Hypnosis LLC	(605) 940-8389	www.healwithhypnosis.com/	Hypnotherapy
WellSpring Therapy Center	(605) 335-1516	www.wellspringtherapysf.com/	Humanistic
OpenDoor, LLC	(605) 250-4455	www.opendoor.website/	Cognitive Behavioral Therapy
Integrative Wellness	(605) 271-1348	www.integrativewellnesssd.com/	Integrative or Holistic Therapy
Kimberly Keiser & Associates Counseling	(605) 644-6907	www.kimberlykeiser.com/	Trauma-Focused Cognitive Behavioral Therapy (TF-CBT)
TN			
Prana Mind Body Healing	(615) 475-8336	www.pranarelaxation.com/	Hypnotherapy
Imago Relationship Therapist	(404) 444-1058	jeannieingram.com/	Humanistic
Mindful Therapy Nashville	(615) 988-0488	www.mindfultherapynashville.com/	Cognitive Behavioral Therapy
A Sense of Place Holistic Therapy &			Integrative

	Counseling Services			
	New Life Counseling & Trauma Therapy, PLLC	(865) 771-0350	therapyfortrauma.com/	Trauma-Focused Cognitive Behavioral Therapy (TF-CBT)
TX	Evolve Hypnosis	(817) 600-9351	www.fwhypnosis.com/	Hypnotherapy
	Healing Hearts Therapy Center	(719) 260-1221	www.healingheartstherapy.net/Services.html	Humanistic
	Dallas Whole Life Counseling	(972) 755-0996	dallaswholelife.com/	Cognitive Behavioral Therapy
	Positive Soul Holistic Therapy	(210) 858-6127	positivesoultherapy.com/	Integrative or Holistic Therapy
UT	Celeste Smith Therapy	(903) 287-0780	celestesmiththerapy.com/	Trauma-Focused Cognitive Behavioral Therapy (TF-CBT)
	Success WOW!	(385) 234-8375	www.successwow.com/	Hypnotherapy
	Simple Modern Therapy	(801) 920-7112	simplemodern.org/	Humanistic
	Mindset Family Therapy	(801) 427-1054	mindsetfamilytherapy.com/	Cognitive Behavioral Therapy
	Healing			

	Pathways Therapy Center	m/	or Holistic Therapy
VT	Trauma Focused Recovery PLLC	(801) 821-4578	traumafocusedrecovery.com/	Trauma-Focused Cognitive Behavioral Therapy (TF-CBT)
	Motivation Hypnosis	(802) 891-4348	www.motivationhypnosis.com/	Hypnotherapy
	Riverstone Counseling	(802) 864-7423 x310	www.spectrumvt.org/	Humanistic
	Puja Gupta Senning, Therapeutic Coaching, LLC	(802) 353-9062	www.pujacoaching.com/	Cognitive Behavioral Therapy
	The Wellness Collective	(802) 540-0186	wellnesscollectivevt.com/	Integrative or Holistic Therapy
VA	Vermont Counseling & Wellness	(802) 878-4991	www.vermontcounselingandwellness.com/	Trauma-Focused Cognitive Behavioral
	It's Not Therapy	(703) 288-0400	hollowreedhealing.com/	Hypnotherapy
	Live Laugh & Love Life Coaching & Mediation	(757) 941-4104	www.balancelifecoaching.org/	Humanistic
	Lotus of Life Counseling, LLC	(540) 693-0466	www.lotusoflifecounseling.com/	Cognitive Behavioral Therapy
	Aura Holistic			Integrative

	Counseling, PLLC			or Holistic Therapy
	Insight Counseling of Alexandria, LLC	(703) 457-6828	insightcounselingalexandria.com/	Trauma-Focused Cognitive Behavioral Therapy (TF-CBT)
WA	Heartfelt Counseling & Hypnotherapy	(509) 448-5660	heartfelthypnosis.com/	Hypnotherapy
	Salveo Counseling Center	(425) 868-5777	www.salveocounseling.com/	Humanistic
	Acorns Counseling	(425) 215-1328	www.acornscounseling.com/	Cognitive Behavioral Therapy
	Heart of Wellness	(360) 570-0401	heartofwellness.org/	Integrative or Holistic Therapy
	Cassie Uribe, Clinical Social Worker/Therapist	(253) 466-7445	cassieuribe.com/	Trauma-Focused Cognitive Behavioral Therapy (TF-CBT)
WV	Modern Hypnosis Works	(540) 454-0213	modernhypnosisworks.com/	Hypnotherapy
	Whole Brain Solutions, LLC	(304) 826-2194	www.wholebrainsolutionswv.com/	Humanistic
	Dayspring			Cognitive

Counseling Center, Inc.			Behavioral Therapy
Natural Resilience, LLC	(304) 381-2211	www.naturalresilience.org/	Integrative or Holistic Therapy
Apex Counseling	(304) 381-3659	apexcounseling.org/	Trauma-Focused Cognitive Behavioral Therapy (TF-CBT)

WI

Lifestyle By Choice	(608) 213-3158	www.addictionshypnosis.com/	Hypnotherapy
Hillary Counseling, LLC	(414) 333-9969	www.hillarycounseling.com/	Humanistic
Hartford Counseling	(262) 223-6125	www.hartfordcounselingwi.com/	Cognitive Behavioral Therapy
Nourishing Eden Holistic Counseling & Therapeutic Services	(920) 213-1841	nourishingeden.com/	Integrative or Holistic Therapy
Connections Counseling	(608) 233-2100	connectionscounseling.com/	Trauma-Focused Cognitive Behavioral Therapy (TF-CBT)

WY

Seeds Of			

	Change LLC			
	Better Life Counseling LLC	(307) 630-4644	www.betterlife-counseling.com/	Humanistic
	Northern Star Counseling	(307) 421-9329	www.northernstarcounseling.com/	Cognitive Behavioral Therapy
	Peace Love & Reiki/Joy-Life	(307) 315-3610	www.joyoflifeunlimited.com/	Integrative or Holistic Therapy
	Internal Peace Therapy	(307) 414-8581	www.internalpeacetherapy.com/	Trauma-Focused Cognitive Behavioral Therapy (TF-CBT)
DC	District Hypnosis	(202) 853-8400	www.districthypnosis.com/	Hypnotherapy
	Human Revolutions, LLC	(202) 759-2447	humanrevolutions.com/	Humanistic
	The Crone Esquivel Group, LLC	(202) 919-8281	www.croneesquivelgroupllc.com/rose-shelton	Cognitive Behavioral Therapy
	Full Circle Creative Healing	(202) 966-8230	fullcirclecreativehealing.com/holistic-counseling/	Integrative or Holistic Therapy
	Potential Counseling	(202) 798-1380	www.potentialcounseling.com/	Trauma-Focused Cognitive Behavioral Therapy (TF-CBT)
PR	Centro de Crecimiento			

	Gaviota Instituto de Desarrollo Integral y Evaluación	(787) 364-9880	www.consejeria.net/index.html	Humanistic
	Alexandra Ramos Duchateau, Ph.D.	(787) 565-9957	www.psychologypr.com/	Cognitive Behavioral Therapy
	Mark Jimerson, MSW, LICSW	(844) 421-9710	www.jimersonarts.org/	Integrative or Holistic Therapy
STT - VI	Instituto de Desarrollo Integral y Evaluación	(787) 364-9880	www.consejeria.net/	Trauma-Focused Cognitive Behavioral Therapy (TF-CBT)
	Beautiful Dreamers	(340) 473-5146	www.beautifuldreamers.org/	Cognitive Behavioral Therapy
STJ - VI	Synergy Fitness and Wellness Center	(340) 714-2348	www.synergyvi.com/	Integrative or Holistic Therapy
	Fresh Ideas, Inc.	(971) 256-6267	www.ruthbettelheim.com/	Humanistic
	Mind/Body Health & Psychology, LLC	(855) 807-1805	www.mindbodyvi.com/	Cognitive Behavioral Therapy